A framework for the study of linguistics

A framework for the study of linguistics

Albert Weideman

University of the Free State

PAIDEIA PRESS
2011

Copyright © 2011
PAIDEIA PRESS
2123 Godwin Ave S.E.
Grand Rapids, MI 49507
USA
reformationalpublishingproject.com

and

VAN SCHAIK PUBLISHERS
1064 Arcadia Street
Hatfield, 0083
Pretoria
South Africa

ISBN 978-0-88815-209-1

CONTENTS

Chapter 5 The analysis of discourse in English

Chapter 6 Conversation analysis and the maintenance of talk

Chapter 7 A complex systems approach and language

Chapter 8 Linguistic primitives as framework for linguistics

Bibliography

Foreword

How do undergraduate students make sense of their initial encounters with a discipline? How do they collaboratively, with lecturers and peers, actually achieve an introduction to a certain field? How do they then proceed to become intrigued with its analyses and findings? In my experience, the haphazard way in which they initially encounter academic disciplines – more often than not in bits and pieces, in unrelated and incoherent formats – merely contributes to the difficulties they experience in coming to a reasonable understanding of a discipline. Surely bewilderment is not what we want for them? What we actually want to achieve is to enable them not only to understand, but also to go beyond that, in acquiring the ability to interpret what is happening in a certain field.

Such interpretation has two sides. First, it needs an idea of how all of the various subdisciplines within a field cohere. In the case of linguistics, it means seeing the connections between phonology, morphology, syntax, semantics, pragmatics, discourse and text analysis, to name a few. Second, to interpret the developments within a field competently, one needs a sense of its history. Mainstream work within a discipline undergoes several paradigm shifts within the working life of a single academic. How to evaluate and assess the relative merits of such paradigm shifts is a necessary task in any responsible approach to linguistics, or in any other field, for that matter. The alternative is for academics to fall victim to every new perspective or style of analysis, or to remain firmly in the grip of the paradigm in which they were trained. Surely neither is a satisfactory or responsible way of engaging with a discipline?

This book has grown out of my experience, over 40 years, of making sense of linguistics within a certain framework. My engagement with the field has for most of this time been from the perspective of a deliberately foundational, philosophical framework. Its first premise is that we would not have had a discipline of linguistics if its field of study was not circumscribed by the lingual mode of experience. Its further premise is almost beguilingly simple: nothing is absolute, and everything is connected with everything else. Though unique, the lingual dimension is therefore not absolute, but connected with all other aspects of reality. The conceptual elaboration of this framework has, furthermore, given me a sense that linguistics is not many disciplines, but one, however much we wish to divide it up into formal ('theoretical') and sociolinguistic camps. Indeed, in many recent approaches to linguistic analysis – systemic functional grammar, cognitive linguistics and a complex systems approach – we find attempts to articulate a sense of wholeness within the discipline.

The trouble is: these newer approaches often utilise older styles of analysis. In a complex systems approach, for example, thick ethnographic description and conversation analysis may form the building blocks of the new paradigm, that make possible and lead to further interpretation within it. To teach only a complex systems approach to linguistics without dealing with older styles of analysis is to risk ignorance of less recent styles without which the new cannot exist.

We therefore need both historical and systematic sense. That is what a framework such as the one utilised here seeks to provide. In an earlier book, *Beyond expression: A systematic study of the foundations of linguistics* (Weideman, 2009), I have tried to articulate the systematic and historical dimensions of linguistics in an academically responsible way. That book, however, was written for an audience that is already well versed in the field. It may therefore be less accessible to newcomers. Given the primary audience this book is aimed at, second and third year students of

English on courses of study that are already packed to the brim with all manner of other offerings, I have been forced not only to write in a more accessible style, but also to make a fairly ruthless selection of the topics and paradigms that should be included in such an introductory textbook. That selection may easily be contested, and I would be the first to agree that it is partial, being sensitive in the first instance to our own institutional context and expertise.

The main point that this book tries to make, however, is that it is possible to entertain a vision that linguistics is a single, whole discipline. That is a perspective that is well worth adopting, since it looks to a discipline that is intelligible because it is whole, despite being rich in its paradigmatic variety and in entertaining different systematic emphases. It is also a view that is worth nurturing because it looks to the future. It brings a sense of understanding to linguistics that makes doing it academically sustainable, and likely to be useful beyond the shifts in perspective that today's emerging young linguists will no doubt experience in their academic lifetimes. The framework for linguistics described in this book is an invitation to those entering the discipline to become intrigued by things lingual. Without that single-minded focus it is hard to imagine entry into the ranks of those who professionally call themselves linguists.

Albert Weideman
Bloemfontein

January 2010

1 What is linguistics?

Fields of study, academic disciplines, and their foundations

Many students arrive in their final year of study with no clear idea of how their fields of study are defined, or how these fields relate to other fields. Nor do they know how the variety of academic fields of study that they have encountered in their studies relates to the world outside of the university. Yet it is for this world, or for the study of an aspect or dimension of it that the university is supposed to prepare them. If it wishes to serve well the academic and professional needs of its students, a university and the opportunities for study that it affords cannot leave them with a sense that all that they have learned are bits and pieces. Such scatterings of insight and analysis, unrelated not only to the future needs of students, but often unrelated to other academic fields, or, in the worst case, unrelated even to components within a single field, are neither what students need nor what they rightfully deserve.

The argument of this course is that students are being done a disservice if their encounter with a field of study is offered in piecemeal fashion, and incoherently. This course will therefore set out as clearly as it can a framework for linguistic study. This framework will serve as the foundation from which we can survey all of linguistics. It will allow us to make sense of its many sub-disciplines, and enable us to see how linguistics relates to other fields, as well as beyond the academy to our professional lives after graduation.

A field of study in the academic side of our world is called a discipline. We speak of the discipline of mathematics, the discipline of physics, the discipline of sociology, the discipline of economics, or, in our case, the discipline of linguistics. By calling these fields disciplines, we emphasise in the notion of 'field' not only that it has limits, boundaries, and demarcation, but also add to it an idea that different fields will have diverse content, and potential variation in what is considered an acceptable way of analysing things in a certain domain. We can only make sense of disciplines if we have a way of demarcating them as such, and as different from others in various respects. This is another way of saying that to know what a discipline is and what it involves, we need to define it. Added to this, such a definition must define our field, linguistics, in such a way that it is clearly different from other fields.

These kinds of issues are philosophical ones. So when the term 'framework' or 'foundation' is used in this course, it means that we are addressing questions related to the philosophical groundwork or basis of our field, linguistics. It is important to note that these foundational questions and their answers are not linguistics. They cannot be answered merely by reference to linguistic distinctions, our analytical methods, or components of the field. They are philosophical or foundational in nature.

If we do not answer them, however, our linguistic work itself will lack coherence and meaning, and will become a piecemeal exercise. Of course, if we are certain that what we wish to do is linguistics, we may be tempted to rush in headlong, considering how to learn to *do* linguistics a much greater priority than standing back and first answering some philosophical questions. It is this urgency that may understandably have created an unwillingness or inability among those who teach and do linguistics to answer first some critically important questions. The point is: if we do not take the time to clarify the framework issues first, they may come back to haunt us later. Worse, the lack of answers to foundational questions at the outset may make us uncritical victims of the latest academic fashions in our disciplines, with no theoretical equipment at our disposal with which to evaluate the merits or weaknesses of a new approach. The only antidote to becoming a victim of what is currently academically fashionable is to take the philosophical foundations of linguistics seriously. What is currently the most prominent approach may have fallen – indeed will fall, for it is certain to happen – into disfavour in the future, just when we may be in need of linguistic insight and distinctions. To hear that an approach is out of date just when you need it most, and to have no tools for assessing what it has been replaced with, is an unenviable position for any language professional to be in. For our future professional needs, we want to have a framework that will enable us to assess the merits and demerits of each new approach that appears on the horizon of linguistic distinction-making.

There are three related philosophical questions that we must answer before embarking on doing linguistics. The answers to these questions will serve as our guides when we enter the field. The first question is: How do we define linguistics? The second one is: How does linguistics relate to other disciplines? And the final question is: How does linguistic work relate to our professional lives?

In what follows below, I shall make use freely of the distinctions and insights in my study of the foundations of linguistics (Weideman, 2009).

The definition of a discipline

Academic disciplines are defined by their study of a unique dimension of our experience. Dimensions or facets of experience are not concrete things, but aspects of things. As we shall see below, if we try to define disciplines in terms of concrete phenomena, we run into a multitude of theoretical controversies and contradictions. The aspects of concrete things, such as a house, a tree, a dog, or a statue, a book, a painting, or a coin, are theoretically distinguishable dimensions of those things. Each concrete thing, including language, when we view it as an object, features a number of unique aspects. For example, a tree has a numerical dimension (it is a single tree), a spatial facet (it occupies a piece of land), an organic aspect (it is a growing and living thing), and a social dimension (it stands in a park, where people may use its shade for recreation), to name but a few. It may even have an historical side (a tree planted in commemoration of an important event), or an aesthetic one (it may be pleasing to the eye, or might function as a symbol in a work of art), or a juridical dimension (for example when it becomes the centre of a dispute between neighbours), or have economic value (it can be cut down and sold). Though this is unlikely to be factually true, an apple tree reputedly helped Newton think through his theory of gravity, so trees may, in their interaction with humans, exhibit a logical side. Of course, they also possess a physical one, which is evident when we chop them down to use for fuel.

All of the distinguishable dimensions of our experience yield the unique aspects that help us to define theoretical disciplines. These aspects are the following (with their unique or defining kernel in brackets): the numerical (discreteness), spatial (extension), kinematic (regular movement), physical (energy-effect), biotic (organic life), psychical (feeling), logical (analysis), historical (formative power), lingual (expression by means of signs), social (interaction), economic (frugality), aesthetic (harmony), juridical (retribution), ethical (love) and faith (belief).

It is easy to see how these provide the defining moments that enable us to distinguish between, respectively, mathematics (defined by the study of the numerical and spatial aspects), physics (kinematic dimension), chemistry (the study of energy-effect), biology (biotic dimension), psychology (feelings and emotion), and then logic, history, linguistics, sociology, economics, aesthetics, jurisprudence, ethics, and theology.

It is also apparent that some of these disciplines belong to what we may call the natural sciences, and others to the so-called human or cultural sciences. The natural sciences study the natural dimensions of our world, such as the numerical, the spatial, the kinematic, the physical, the organic and the psychical. The cultural disciplines focus on the dimensions that are characteristically human: the logical, the historical, the lingual, the social, the juridical, and so on.

Each aspect therefore provides a guarantee of the uniqueness of the discipline involved. It provides us with an angle from which we can proceed to form concepts of phenomena within a certain domain. If the dimensions of our experience were themselves not unique, each with an irreducible, defining nuclear moment, they would not have been theoretically distinguishable, and if they were not distinguishable, we would have lacked a theoretical and philosophical basis for distinguishing between various disciplines.

If these aspects of our experience allow us to distinguish and demarcate disciplinary boundaries, they may also show us how linguistics as a discipline is related to other fields. Let's consider this below, by first looking at answers to the second and third questions posed above, before returning subsequently to a more detailed answer to the first ("What is linguistics?").

The relationship between linguistics and other disciplines

Not only are the aspects that define the fields of study of the various disciplines unique, each with their own irreducible kernel or defining moment, but they are at the same time inextricably related and intertwined. Each unique aspect analogically reflects others. This analogical reflection is a reference, taken from the vantage point of one aspect, to another aspect of experience.

Take as an example the lingual dimension of experience, which shall be occupying us if we are doing linguistics, and consider how it reflects or refers to other dimensions of experience. When, from a uniquely lingual point of view, we look at the numerical dimension of our world, we see a *unity within a multiplicity of lingual rules and lingual facts*, which is called a lingual system. The analogy or reference should be clear: the concept of "unity within multiplicity" is an originally numerical concept. When we refer to it from a lingual point of view, we are able to conceptualise "lingual unity within multiplicity", or what in linguistics is called *lingual systems*.

It is one of the tasks of linguistic enquiry to show how a variety of lingual systems interact, and at different levels (of sound, form, meaning, and so forth). For example, in the sound system of English, there are three ways of regularly forming the plural: with the sounds /z/, /s/ and /iz/. The sound system of the language therefore allows three different sounds when regular English plurals are formed. From the vantage point of the level where they are formed, we speak not of phonemes, which are units of sound, but of morphemes, small lingual units or forms that are lingually significant. At this level, the sound system combines with the morpheme system to allow us to form plurals such as *bars, facts*, and *voices* from the singulars *bar, fact* and *voice*, by adding the morpheme |s| to each. A single meaningful lingual form or morpheme (|s|) allows us to form the three regular plurals, and we articulate this in sound by means of adding the sounds /-z/, /-s/ and /-iz/ to the three root morphemes (*bar, fact* and *voice*). The lingual sound system and lingual form system interact, or become a unity within a multiplicity of (in this case: two) interacting systems. The regularly available sounds (/z/, /s/ and /iz/) interact with the forms to create additional lingually meaningful units. We observe here not only a multiplicity of rule systems at various levels, but also a multiplicity of factual lingual units that are governed by these systems.

Moreover, the multiplicity of the interacting systems is illustrated further when we note that in each case we have a distinguishable new word, with a regularly distinguishable relation (plural : singular) to the original root form. Thus, in addition to sound system and form system, there is a system operating at the level of meaning: a *bar*, a *fact* and a *voice* are words in the singular that are systematically different in meaning from their plurals *bars, facts*, and *voices*.

The example is designed to show that there are often multiple interacting lingual systems. In this case we have chosen to look at the interaction between only three lingual systems: a sound system, a morphemic system (operating at the level of form) and a semantic one (operating at the level of meaning).

Of course, language operates at many more levels and states than the ones we have theoretically isolated for scrutiny here. In fact, one of the most exciting new developments for linguistics and language related disciplines, complex systems theory (Larsen-Freeman & Cameron, 2008), stresses in particular the interaction not only of lingual systems and subsystems, but also how these in turn interact with developmental, cognitive, social, and other systems.

As a second example, consider how the lingual dimension of experience analogically reflects the spatial aspect, which is characterised by extension or continuity. When we speak of the lingual range of meaning of a word, we can express that range in terms of a field, as has been done in semantic field theory (cf. Van Heerden, 1965: 70ff.). So, for example, the meaning of the word *dark* can overlap in part with that of *dusk* and *black*, and can be graphically represented thus:

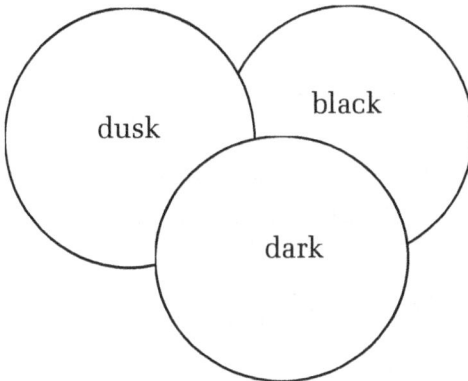

Figure 1: Overlapping lingual ranges of meaning

Overlapping and non-overlapping meanings on these lingual fields or ranges of meaning can be illustrated in the following examples:

(a) It was already dark / dusk [but not *black*] when he got home.
(b) When he got home he was in a dark / black [but not *dusk*] mood.

This expression of the field of meaning of a word can be used, for instance, to plot the ranges of meaning of synonyms or near synonyms, like those derived from the three main sources of the English lexicon, such as *rise* (from Old English), *mount* (from French) and *ascend* (from Latin), or, again from the same three major sources, *ask, question* and *interrogate* (for these and other examples, cf. Crystal, 2003: 124). If we plot the near-synonymous meanings of these as semantic fields, we are likely to see more overlapping than non-overlapping lingual ranges. Or consider, also adapted from Crystal (2003: 213), how one can spatially plot the semantic or lingual ranges of prepositions in terms of five parameters: destination or position indicated; or reference to a point, surface or volume:

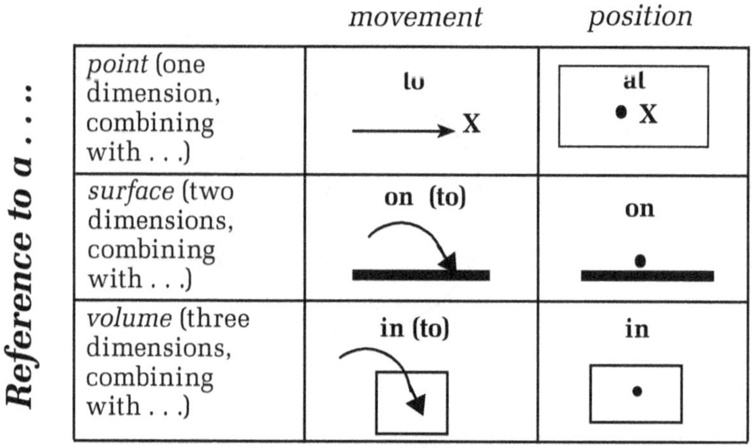

		movement	*position*
Reference to a . . . :	*point* (one dimension, combining with . . .)	tu ———▶ X	at • X
	surface (two dimensions, combining with . . .)	on (to)	on •
	volume (three dimensions, combining with . . .)	in (to)	in •

Figure 2: The lingual ranges of some prepositions

As a third example of analogies in the lingual aspect, consider how in English morphology we have more than one system of lingual means (rules) by which that language has created and can continue to create new forms. By adding one particular kind of morpheme, a suffix, we can extend the meaning of a noun in forming its plural, in the regular case, by adding –s, as in *dogs, plates, drinks*. This is a lingual extension of the meaning of the word, from singular to plural. Or, again in the regular case, by adding the morpheme –*ed* to a verb, we can extend its meaning to indicate the past tense, as in *walked, talked, kicked*. The concept of lingual extension is clearly an analogical spatial linguistic concept.

The spatial analogy within the lingual dimension of reality that we are focussing on here is evident not only in the notion of lingual extension, but also in those of lingual position and sequence. In these examples, it is clear that, in order to create a regular plural as in the examples above, the root (*dog, plate, drink*) in each case has to occur first in sequence, and the suffix in the final position. There is a prescribed sequence (root + suffix), as in the formation of regular past tense.

This sequencing or ordering of discrete elements, which in this case is a sequence of morphemes, is of course the life-blood of mathematics (cf. how the natural numbers are ordered in the sequence of 1 before 2, 2 before 3, 3 before 4, and so on). Yet, in considering in all of these examples the concepts of discreteness, position, sequence and extension, we have been pursuing linguistic, not mathematical, matters. We have been looking at numerical and spatial concepts from a lingual angle.

There are many more examples of a similar nature that one might give. So, for example, in the concept of *lingual regularity* (in the formation of plurals and the past tense in English, but also in the consistent relationships between singular and plural, or present tense and past tense) we encounter, within the lingual dimension of experience that we have taken as a vantage point, an echo of the kinematic aspect of our world. Similarly, we may discover in concepts like *lingual power, lingual development, lingual cognition, lingual identity* or *meaning, lingual form*, and so on, echoes within the lingual dimension of, respectively, the spheres of energy-effect, organic growth, the psychical aspect, the logical, the formative, etc.

All of these echoes mean that the lingual aspect of our experience is related analogically to all other dimensions of reality. By extension, it means that the field of investigation of linguistics is linked in principle to the fields of investigation of all other disciplines. This ties in strongly with the notion not only that our experience is one, but also that our entire scientific endeavour is related and potentially coherent. Academic activity, in whatever field, is in principle integral and whole. It is clear that linguistics is therefore related to other disciplines, but is also unique, and that this uniqueness is guaranteed by the fact that the view it takes of things is a lingual view (as distinct from a kinematic, or physical, or psychological, or historical, or even social one). We return to this point below in the form of a number of arguments when we specifically set out to define linguistics.

The relationship of linguistics to our future professional needs

The third question that needs to be answered before we embark on linguistic study is how it relates to our future professional needs.

The answer that will be given here is preliminary, since the professional needs of students are likely to vary substantially. Moreover, in order to have a clear grasp of how linguistics can assist one professionally, one of course needs to know more about linguistics than one does at the outset. A proper answer can only be given if one is much more familiar with the content and methodologies of linguistic distinction-making.

Most students who take up the study of linguistics will, however, have an interest in language that will endure into their professional lives. And the professions are probably what we may call the language professions, or the work of language practitioners. Our students of linguistics are likely to end up as language teachers, translators, interpreters, editors, journalists, lexicographers, speech pathologists and therapists, curriculum or test designers, and the like.

For each of these professions their initial linguistics training matters, for in each of these fields linguistic distinctions often lie at the basis of work that is done there. For example, a lexicographer will depend on some definition of what a word or a lexeme is, and this definition is likely to be derived from some linguistic insight or distinction, that in its turn derives from a particular philosophical approach to linguistics. Defining a word is not at all straightforward, and isolating it from a stream of sound, even when recorded, can be extremely difficult. We may all know how to isolate perceptually, and hear or read English words, but think for a moment how difficult it is to hear words in a strange language. What we may hear as words, may be merely 'chunks' of language that consist either of one or of several words. So someone learning English, for example, who knows very little of the language, encountering both the questions "What's the use of complaining?" and "What's the use of worrying?" may be forgiven for thinking that *What's the use of* may be a single word. Indeed, Reichling (cf. Reichling, 1947) is generally credited for giving the first theoretically valid definition of a word in his doctoral thesis, written a mere 80 years ago. This does not mean that words were indistinguishable before, but simply that their theoretical delimitation before then left much to be desired.

In similar fashion, language teachers will, consciously or unconsciously, use materials that are based on linguistic distinctions or linguistic theory. In one recent development in Australian schools, language course designers explicitly made use of Halliday's systemic functional grammar (cf. Halliday, 1978, 1985; Berry, 1975; Butler, 1985) in their curriculum design of language courses for the newly literate.

Other applications include the study of stylistic and discourse similarity and variation that will facilitate the identification of evidence within the study of forensic linguistics, an important and growing sub-field. Or take the use of theories of language competence that are employed by those who develop language tests. In fact, much of the validity of a language test depends on

11

the theoretical defensibility of the construct or model of language ability on which it is based.

Speech therapists and pathologists are further users of linguistic distinctions and theories, as are corpus linguists who collect large samples of the language, often for computer analysis. Such analysis is preceded by the development of a sound theoretical linguistic basis. There are already corpora consisting of more than 450 million English words (Crystal, 2003: 448), and there are indications that these large collections of data may be the stimulus for new analyses and insights into the workings of the English language in the present century. It is an exciting time to become involved in linguistics.

Despite these examples of how theoretical linguistic distinctions are used, however, linguistic insight cannot merely be applied wholesale to any language problem. Indeed, though there is a separate discipline of "applied linguistics", it is wrong to think that it is similar to or merely an extension of linguistics, or that it simply takes a linguistic insight that can in some fashion be related to any and all language problems and issues. The relationship between linguistics and applied linguistics is much more complex, and merits separate discussion, for two good reasons.

The first is that linguistic insight has not only been beneficial, but in some cases has been disadvantageous to the solution of language problems. The second is that thinking of linguistics as something that can be 'applied' brings us back to the now discredited intellectual arrogance associated with trends in scientific thinking that pretend that 'scientific' solutions are necessarily the best, and always the most authoritative. In the postmodern times that we live, such modernist pretence has not only come under intense scrutiny, but its validity as scientific 'truth' has been thoroughly discredited. Indeed, since the time of the Enlightenment there has been in Western scientific thought a tendency to ascribe to scientific analysis and investigation the ultimate power, that will lead us through progressive discovery to the truth. As I remark elsewhere (Weideman, 2009: 1), this belief in an all-powerful 'science' is an enduring myth of modernism:

One of the die-hard myths of modern thought is the so-called neutrality or objectivity of our subjective theorizing. It is a dogma of scientific endeavor that has survived almost every major shake-up in the history of Western thinking. But it is nonetheless recognized today more than ever before that the dogma of objectivity is exactly that: an unverified and indeed unverifiable dogma. It has remained as much an illusion as the intellectual mirage of the attendant belief in the progressive discovery of truth.

Of course, as Robins (1967: 3) remarks:

It is tempting, and flattering to one's contemporaries, to see the history of a science as the progressive discovery of truth and the attainment of the right methods. But this is a fallacy. The aims of a science vary in the course of its history, and the search for objective standards by which to judge the purposes of different periods is apt to be an elusive one. 'The facts' and 'the truth' are not laid down in advance, like the solution to a crossword puzzle, awaiting the completion of discovery. Scientists themselves do much to determine the range of facts, phenomena, and operations that fall within their purview, and they themselves set up and modify the conceptual framework within which they make what they regard as significant statements about them.

Much the same point is made by Palmer (1976: 16) when he says that "in linguistics ... the facts are so intangible ... Indeed what we consider as facts will to a large extent depend on the framework, i.e. the model within which we describe them."

So linguistics has limits, and therefore probably possesses only a limited and humble role in all of our future professional lives. That does not mean that its role is unimportant, nor that we should not take its insights very seriously. But linguists and applied linguists, the latter group being those who focus on designing solutions for language problems, will do well to stay abreast of trends and approaches in linguistics lest they fall victim to those trends instead of being able to use them with deliberation and sophistication.

Having considered how linguistics relates to other disciplines and given a preliminary indication of how it may impact on our professional lives, we return now to a more detailed discussion of the first question: what is linguistics?

The definition of linguistics

It is not difficult or uncommon to find in an introductory book on linguistics a definition of the field such as

(1) Linguistics is the study of language (Berry, 1975: 1).

Clearly, such a definition is not only vague (and therefore immediately needs a number of qualifications), but it is also highly problematic in the context of what is actually done by scholars working in the field today. As a definition, it does not distinguish, for example, between, on the one hand, those who study a language or languages other than their own for the sake of becoming fluent in them (the earlier meaning of 'linguist'), and, on the other, someone who views the study of language not as a practical skill that must be acquired, but as a theoretical study in its own right.

All right then, we may say, there are linguists and linguists. If the conventional dictionary definition does not make this distinction, indiscriminately calling both of these 'linguists' rather than reserving the term for those persons who study a (foreign) language or languages for the sake of acquiring them, and coining a second term, say 'linguistician', for the ones who go about their business in a theoretically disciplined way, then surely the only alteration to make to our definition (1) would be to insert some reference to the theoretical interests of the second group. So, not surprisingly, another common definition of linguistics that we find is the following:

(2) Linguistics may be defined as the scientific study of language (as, e.g., in Lyons, 1969: 1).

But does this solve our problem?

As anyone who works as a "theoretical linguist" knows, it is not infrequent that one is assailed with questions by friends and acquaintances on language problems that may only be remotely connected with current theoretical interests in the field. Nonetheless, to the layman, someone who does 'linguistics' is a professional, an expert who should be able to confirm that children are better than adults at learning a second language,[1] or who should know why it is that a three year old son of a neighbour does not yet speak, or a ten year old daughter of an acquaintance has begun to stutter. If one is also teaching linguistics within a language department at university, one is, moreover, inundated with enquiries as to what would be 'correct' forms of that language, what the spelling of certain words might be, and so forth, since it is clearly assumed that a linguist is an authoritative source on these matters. Again, though, we might argue, all these popular conceptions of what linguistics is – some of which are in fact nothing but misconceptions – are not adequate objections to our definition (2), specifically because many of these questions are indeed studied in some linguistic sub-field, and thus (2) should be allowed to stand, be it then with some qualifications.

This would have been a perfectly valid conclusion if linguistics had been the only academic discipline with an interest in language. But this is demonstrably not the case. To someone who studies acoustic physics, for example, human language sounds may be of particular interest; the technical applications of such knowledge in the fields of architecture and electronic engineering

---

1. Contrary to popular belief ("folk linguistics"), it is by no means certain that this is true. There is some hard evidence in studies that have been conducted to point to the exact reverse, viz. that adults are in fact better than children. There might be a "crucial age" before which one must try to learn a second or foreign language, but this may, according to some earlier studies, be closer to 30 (when we are certainly no longer children) than 7, 10, 14 or any of the other magical dates that are often mentioned (cf. Cook, 1978: 80ff., van Els *et al.*, 1984: 108f.). Moreover, the acceptance nowadays of a number of different accents and a variety of 'Englishes' instead of one pure standard for all has made the 'problem' of the retention of an accent into adulthood less prominent.

alone make scientific study of the acoustic properties of human speech a worthwhile undertaking. Likewise theologians are for their part often concerned with the scientific study of human language, specifically the study of what we might call certitudinal discourse, i.e. the language of 'ultimates', be it in the Bible, the revered books of other faiths, or in confessional texts generally. Similarly, too, jurisprudence has always been centrally interested in the interpretation of stretches of language in legal texts in order to interpret them properly; psychology in the scientific analysis of the patient's talk in psychotherapy; mathematics in the theoretical interpretation of the language of algebraic formulae, etc. Yet none of these disciplines in any but the widest sense has the same focus as linguistics, and, as scientific disciplines, seem to be quite distinct from it. The problem, therefore, as one linguist has put it, is that

> the phenomena of language can be studied from different points of view. Dozens of sciences can study linguistic phenomena ... from as many points of view – each one putting these phenomena into relation with phenomena of some other sort. What aspect of the phenomena, if any, is left to linguistics as its exclusive property? (Wells, 1966: 15)

In desperation, one might very well ask if there is then any valid reason for attempting to define linguistics, if even an apparently sound definition such as (2) obviously needs to be modified and qualified before one can arrive at a rational conclusion, i.e. find the "aspect of the phenomena" which is the exclusive concern of linguistics. If, however, linguistics should indeed, as another famous structuralist linguist (Hjelmslev, 1963: 5f.) put it

> attempt to grasp language, not as a conglomerate of non-linguistic (e.g., physical, physiological, psychological, logical, sociological) phenomena, but as a self-sufficient totality, a structure *sui generis*

then its definition, in terms of a unique, characterizing aspect of language, remains crucially important. So the perplexing question of whether we should perhaps abandon any attempt at defining linguistics – in favour of simply getting on with doing linguistics–

remains. As the history of the discipline of linguistics has shown time and again, however, too much depends on one's (explicit or implicit) view of what linguistics is for this question to be left in abeyance. The answer to this question has a direct bearing on what aspect of language one wishes to focus linguistic enquiry.

In the foregoing, I have been hinting that linguistic study may perhaps be defined by what the language theorist wishes to focus on, i.e. by that aspect of the phenomena of language on which linguistic theory is apt to concentrate. An eventual modification of definition (2) might then be

> (3) Linguistics is the theoretical study of an aspect X of
> language (where X has not yet been defined).

A sure way of finding out what 'X' in (3) is, according to some, would be to look at what the data of linguistic enquiry are, for it should be obvious from the data of the theoretical enquiry what the as yet mysterious "aspect X" of language is. So, if we can find a generally accepted view of what the data of linguistic enquiry might be, then, with 'X' in (3) having been identified, the riddle of the definition of linguistics would be solved.

The data of linguistic enquiry

In the prelude to modern linguistics in the 19th century[2] linguistic thinking was centred on the historical lineage of particular languages or groups of languages. Some explanation

---

2. This does not imply that linguistics proper did not exist before this time, but simply that before the 20th century linguistic concept-formation was markedly different. Students who embark upon linguistic study will do well to read an account of pre-modern linguistics (as in Robins, 1967, who devotes more than half of his book to pre-Saussurean linguistics) to acquaint themselves with the history of the discipline. There are numerous reasons for being informed about the history of linguistic thought, not the least being that one very influential recent linguistic theory, transformational-generative grammar, explicitly tries to find its roots in the linguistic thought of the Enlightenment, and that, especially in the case of English, the historical influence of the prescriptive grammarians is by no means a spent force.

had to be offered for the fact that many European languages seemed to be related, and also that in the development of a particular language there were successive historical stages: modern English, for example, had developed from Middle English, which in turn had grown out of Anglo-Saxon. Of prime concern here were the sounds or the phonic stratum of language, and laws were formulated to account for sound shifts occurring between different stages of a language, or even between the oldest known form of a language and a hypothesized proto-form, such as Proto-Indo-European (cf. Sampson, 1980: ch. 1). If any answer had to be given in this period to the question of what 'X' is in our definition (3) above, it would surely have been: the historical aspects of language change, especially as these manifest themselves in successive sound-changes.

That this view did not go unchallenged is evident from the sharp distinction that the founder of modern linguistics, Ferdinand de Saussure, drew between historical linguistics and synchronic linguistics. In the latter kind of linguistics one viewed language as a cross-section of the ongoing process: language was, as it were, frozen to the gaze of the theoretical observer, and in this observed entity the theorist discovered the system of language (or *langue*, in De Saussure's terms). De Saussure's answer as to what constituted 'X' would then have to be: the system(s) through which the signs of language are related. This answer formed the basis of the school of linguistic thinking that came to be known as structuralism or structural(ist) linguistics.

On the surface, the two answers as to what the true data of linguistic enquiry might seem to be quite dissimilar, and indeed they are (even though, for De Saussure, 'system' would also include the – now 'frozen' – sound system of a language). Nor is De Saussure's answer the only possible one. Early transformational grammar held that the data of linguistic enquiry were to be found in the speech (and intuition) of the native speaker of a language. This view, in turn, is being vigorously opposed in current thinking on complex systems theory and language (Larsen-Freeman & Cameron, 2008), which sees the data of enquiry as many interacting lingual and non-lingual systems that combine to become, in an individual, a set of "language resources". Thus, a preliminary look at the history of linguistic theory gives us little hope of finding any firm agreement on the data of linguistics, and of consequently resolving the mystery of what 'X' is in our definition of linguistics.

If we look closely, however, we can see that De Saussure's view of language as a system of signs does give us a more abstract way of characterizing linguistic enquiry. With historical hindsight, we can today see the force of this abstraction operative in linguistics as we came to know it in the 20th century, and how it has continued to influence current work in the field. By isolating or abstracting the 'signalling' aspect of language as its unique characterizing feature, De Saussure has allowed us to see that this is what distinguishes linguistic interest in language from theological, psychological, historical, mathematical or other kinds of interest in language.

Above, I have called this abstract aspect of language the lingual mode of experience. De Saussure would probably have preferred the term 'semiotic', whereas a later structuralist, Greimas, uses the term *modus significandus*. We can then try out this formulation as a means of distinguishing between various ways of experiencing and legitimately analysing language: linguistically, confessionally, psychologically, historically, juridically, and so forth. Then we can make the final alteration to our definition, and say that

(4) Linguistics is the theoretical study of the lingual aspect of language,

where 'lingual' refers to the fact that language is *expression that is related to the understanding of signs*. This definition is by no means perfect, not the least because it is still very general (and hence vague), but at least it is a working hypothesis, and its very generality allows it to capture theoretical linguistic concerns that are quite divergent, as we shall see in the next section.

An encyclopaedic view of the field

One of the strongest points in favour of the very general formulation of the field of linguistic enquiry in (4) above is that it allows us to account for a wide spectrum of differentiated linguistic sub-disciplines.

The linguistic sub-discipline which reaped what were probably the first fruits of the more abstract modern formulation of the field of linguistics was the study of language sounds. Phonetics, as this study was called, had been studied since the time of the Renaissance and had, by the end of the 19th century, become increasingly sophisticated: the IPA (International Phonetic Alphabet) had been formulated, and various applications had been made possible in the technical and educational fields (cf. Robins, 1967: 202ff.). Through the development of the more abstract concept of the phoneme, the foundation was laid for the linguistic sub-discipline known as phonology to grow out of phonetic concerns with the sounds of language.

To see how the theoretical concept of the phoneme differs from that of the more ambiguous term "speech sound", we need to look at the definitions of each. A speech sound is any phonetically distinct unit of sound; thus the English 'clear' (l) as in _long_ and _leg_ and the so-called dark (l) as in _bui_l_d_ and _ve_l_d_ are distinct phonetic units. However, since a phoneme can roughly be defined as a unit of sound that serves to distinguish different words, it seems that we need to distinguish only one phoneme /l/ in English, i.e. an abstract sound unit that has the effect, for example, of distinguishing _land_ from _band_, or _bit_ from _lit_, through its opposition to another phoneme of English, viz. /b/ (Lyons, 1969: 99ff.).[3] Clearly, this is a much more economical way of studying the phonic stratum of language, and facilitates the formulation of generalizations at this level. But the crucial point is that the Saussurean distinction, which differentiates between

---

3. 'Clear' and 'dark' (l) are therefore, on the more abstract phonological level, merely two positional variations of the same phoneme in English (Lyons, 1969: 112). Such positional variants of the same phoneme are called allophones.

the abstract sign system of language (i.e. *langue*, to which the phoneme belongs) and the concrete facts of speech (*parole*, to which the speech sounds belong), had paved the way for the establishment of the linguistic sub-discipline of phonology (Robins, 1967: 204).

This has been one example of the benefits derived from the rather abstract formulation of the field of enquiry of modern linguistics. Without going into any further historical details, let us now take a look at the fields of other linguistic sub-disciplines. Since there has always been a recognition of the hierarchical or 'levelled' character of language, it has been generally accepted in linguistics that sounds combine to form words, words combine to form phrases and clauses, and clauses combine to form sentences.[4] So we find in linguistics, alongside of phonology, various other sub-disciplines. Morphology concentrates on the aspect of word-formation (e.g. how we get the past tense form of a regular verb by adding, in the case of English, an *-ed* morpheme), while syntax investigates the organization of words, phrases and clauses in sentences. In the chapter below that deals with this, you will be taking a hard look at syntactic theory, and during this time one of the possible defects of definition (4) above will become clear: the formulation of the field of linguistic enquiry is so general and vague that not every grammarian would agree as to what the data of syntactic enquiry might be. In fact, there are numerous competing approaches not only to English syntax but in each of the previously mentioned linguistic sub-disciplines, and no definition of a field can (or, for that matter, should) rule out internal differences of opinion or theoretical starting points.

Apart from such conflicting analyses within a linguistic sub-discipline, there have moreover developed a number of other fields within linguistics that claim to be complementary to the study of phonology and syntax. Halliday, for example, claims that the linguistic system operates on at least three levels: apart

---

4. This is a very crude and simplified formulation, but will have to suffice for the present. One point, especially, that could easily be missed here is that the units mentioned are quite abstract – something that a person who is familiar only with their non-technical uses might fail to grasp.

from the phonological level and the lexicogrammatical stratum (which includes syntax, morphology and lexis), there is also a semantic level (Halliday, 1978: 128), which obviously necessitates the study of meaning in the linguistic sub-discipline known as semantics. If we also accept that meaning is not purely sentence-meaning, i.e. meaning in isolation from a social context in which a sentence is uttered, then the way is clear for the development of yet another linguistic sub-discipline, viz. pragmatics.

It is clear that the theoretical knowledge of language gained by phonological and syntactic analyses ought to be complemented by semantic and pragmatic information, though linguists are by no means agreed on the exact nature of this complementarity, or whether it is at all possible to construct such an overall view of language. The philosophical framework that is being used in this course, however, gives a positive answer to this. It claims, in fact, that we need an overall view of how the lingual mode of experience functions in our lives and in our world if we are to make theoretical sense of it.

Together with text linguistics, discourse analysis and conversation analysis, pragmatics forms part of the analyses of language made within the larger sub-discipline of sociolinguistics. These developments have been recent,[5] and attempts to define especially pragmatics have been difficult and even controversial (cf. Levinson, 1983: 1-35), which preclude a definite and precise statement in this regard. Difficult though it may be to define these, what is centrally important in each is the language of conversation, which is regarded as a prototypical manifestation of language (Levinson, 1983: 284f.), as well as the social context in which language is used. On the whole, the growth of the discipline of sociolinguistics has been characterized by the recognition that we do not only speak, but that we speak to each other.

If we could return for a moment to the second definition of linguistics given above, it will now become clear why this definition is only half true: it makes no mention of the speakers

5. An indication of this is the fact that the first textbook on pragmatics (Levinson, 1983) was published a mere twenty-odd years ago.

and producers of language (lingual subjects) and moreover seems to suggest, erroneously, that linguistics is concerned solely with the objective phenomenon of language. If linguistics considered only the lingual object (that which is produced) and wished to exclude from its view lingual subjects (the producers/receivers), then there also would have been no room for psycholinguistics, the linguistic sub-discipline that investigates, amongst other things, the acquisition of language by the human lingual subject, as well as the maturation and possible loss of language (as in aphasic conditions)[6] in the individual. Moreover, if we consider language loss not only from an individual point of view, but from that of a society or whole community whose language is threatened by extinction, it also becomes clear that not only objective lingual facts are within the purview of linguistic thought, but also subjective lingual issues that have social and political dimensions. The theoretical study of the lingual mode of experience can thus be tackled from the angle of either the lingual object or that of the lingual subject, and the generality and abstract character of our definition (4) allows for this possibility.

There is one more issue to be discussed here that will again come into focus during the latter part of the course, and this is the question of whether, in the concepts 'lingual' and 'language', linguistics is restricted to the study of speech, or only to speech and writing, i.e. to verbal language. Most of the recent developments in linguistics, especially in the field of sociolinguistics, have given increasing attention to the lingual, i.e. semiotic or expressive, qualities of gestures that either accompany speech, or, in certain instances, may replace it.

One of the clearest examples of this comes from the field of discourse analysis. One of the fundamental units of analysis here is the concept of lingual 'move' (Coulthard, 1985: 8). What this means, briefly, is that within the space of a single utterance like B's second turn at talk in the following exchange, there may be not only one, but at least two lingual moves by B:

---

6. In respect of this latter concern, the theoretical burden of psycho-linguistics may be shared by neurolinguistics and speech pathology.

A: May I read your message?

B: Yes.

A: Why ... what's it say ... oh that's a ... very sensible thing to say ...

*B: Yes ... Well I'll leave you here for a little longer ...

A: Yes, Brenda ...

(adapted from Svartvik & Quirk, 1980: S.1.8, 376-381, p. 206).

Now, if lingual moves are units of linguistic analysis at the level of discourse, how are we to characterize the moves in an example exchange such as the following:

A: What's the time?

B: ...(pause)... It's five o'clock
(fabricated)

(cf. Goffman, 1981: 41). It can be argued that B's turn at talk, his utterance, again consists of two moves: the first, transcribed here as "... (pause) ...", being his glance at his watch, the second his reply to A's question. We cannot deny that the pause – or specifically the glancing at one's watch – is normally required before giving an answer in cases such as this if we do not wish to express callousness or impoliteness. Here, the gesture or its absence is therefore meaningful or expressive. While some linguists may perhaps still wish to argue whether this gesture is a lingual or a non-lingual move (and for those who restrict 'lingual' to 'verbal' it will certainly be non-lingual), there is no denying in the end that it is indeed expressive, and hence should be part of linguistic investigation according to our definition (4). Even though not enough is known about the gestures that accompany speech, linguistics should not be tied down to a consideration only of verbal phenomena. The lingual dimension of experience that it investigates accommodates all meaningful expression by means of signs, be they in nature verbal (based in sound or print) or non-verbal (based in the bodily musculature).

In conclusion, we might also ask what, in linguistic theory, the status of our present discussion is. Having characterized linguistics and its various sub-disciplines: phonology, morphology, syntax, semantics, sociolinguistics and psycho-linguistics, where does this discussion itself belong? The answer is: we have been discussing the basis of linguistics, its foundations. We may call this kind of undertaking foundational or philosophical linguistics. To use an image that might make the picture somewhat clearer: if our theoretical endeavours can be likened to a house, then linguistics would be one of the rooms, and the study and consideration of what linguistics itself is, i.e. philosophical linguistics, would be the foundations of the room. At the level of philosophical linguistics, one is concerned not so much with the shape or arrangement of the furniture in the room (which would be the tasks of the sub-disciplines of phonology, morphology and syntax) as with the structure of the walls that separate and simultaneously link the room ("linguistic studies") with other rooms (sociology, psychology, hermeneutics, literary theory, history, aesthetics, economics, jurisprudence, etc.).

2 Formal approaches to the description of English: Syntax

The study of form

As we noted in the introductory chapter, the formation of words in English is studied by a linguistic sub-discipline, morphology. While morphology focuses mainly on the processes of lingual formation at word (lexical) level, the remainder of the study of form is conventionally related to the study of lingual structure and formation at sentence or clause level. The study of the latter is known as syntax or grammar, and the task of syntactic theory is to provide the linguist with the most adequate description of whatever language is being studied.

In this section we deal with two approaches to the description of lingual phrase and clause formation in English that have, in various respects, been influential in the development of linguistic studies. We shall merely be scratching the surface here, as it is an almost impossible task to summarize the gist of both transformational-generative grammar and systemic/functional grammar within the space of a few pages. Hence the discussion will inevitably be highly selective, focussing mostly on those features of the two approaches that have a bearing on the subsequent study of linguistics for students of English. For more detailed information on the content of each of these, students are referred to Radford (1981), which is a highly accessible source on transformational grammar, and, in the case of systemic/

functional analysis, to Halliday (1985), which, though formidable in length, is very lucid in exposition.

Whatever their differences in theoretical perspective and stance, the two approaches both have this in common: they constitute attempts to describe the structure of language at the level of **form** (see introduction); they do so, moreover, in terms of abstractly distinguishable, **formal units** of language such as phrase, clause and sentence. Of the two, transformational grammar is certainly the more abstract, and will be discussed first. This syntactic theory has seen numerous versions, from the Standard Theory (Chomsky 1957) to the latest Minimalist version of this grammar (Chomsky 1995), as will be explained below. The one that is dealt with here, the Revised Extended Standard Theory, has been chosen because it is still one of the more accessible versions of this grammar.

Transformational-generative grammar

The year 1957 was, as many commentators on the history of modern linguistics have remarked, a watershed in the development of the discipline. Until then, as the editor of one book observed (Joos, 1966: v), "[d]escriptive linguistics ... seemed ... to be without a serious competitor on our scene..." So on the one hand there was Joos's (1966) book that celebrated the then unchallenged supremacy of a school of linguistic investigation known as American descriptivism, while on the other there was Chomsky's *Syntactic structures* (1957) setting out the embryonic ideas of what eventually became a linguistic revolution that would topple the reign of descriptivism. Transformational-generative grammar had appeared on the scene.

To understand the revolutionary impact of transformational grammar on linguistics, one must take into account its radical departure from some of the most cherished principles of descriptivism. The latter is mainly associated with descriptive studies of the indigenous (Indian) languages of North America. Through the efforts of Leonard Bloomfield to make linguistics an accurate, descriptive science (in the way that this is defined in logical positivism), this brand of American structuralism also became heavily **behaviourist** in its approach (cf. Sampson, 1980: 64ff.).

What this amounted to in the actual description of a language, was that any kind of introspection, i.e. consulting one's own intuitions about language structure, was strictly forbidden; this, to the behaviourist, would create a chaotic state of confusion in any science. Behaviourist linguists therefore went to great lengths to prevent being influenced by any pre-scientific belief, attitude or opinion on language structure that could obscure the unprejudiced observation and subsequent scientific description of the **objective** facts of language. Sampson (1980: 65) relates the example of Charles Fries, who, in writing his grammar of English, avoids even those long-accepted lexical categories of 'noun' and 'verb', preferring rather to call them "Class 1" and "Class 2" words. Any **pre-scientific** interference with the uncluttered and ideally unbiased observation of the facts of language was to be immediately suppressed by behaviourist structuralism as **non-scientific** and not objective. The linguist working in this tradition felt that:

> The folklorist may be interested in Englishmen's beliefs about English; the linguist must concentrate rather on how Englishmen speak when they are not thinking about their language (Sampson, 1980: 66).

Put like this, the behaviourist position seems to be perfectly justified: linguistics, if it is to be a science, must deal with lingual phenomena that are open to observation, accessible to analytical scrutiny and of sufficient generality to be descriptively interesting; since idiosyncratic beliefs and opinions are not susceptible to sensory observation, they fall outside the purview of a linguistics so defined. Indeed, the degree of scientific rigour introduced by behaviourism into linguistic conceptualization has been one of its lasting contributions to the field.

The problem, however, as Chomsky very ably stated in a devastating review of a book by a leading behaviourist psychologist, is that by taking up the extreme position of denying the existence of the mind (since behavioural science should consider only sensorily perceptible phenomena), the behaviourist falls prey to an extremely simplistic view of language: that external stimuli are directly relatable to the output that we call language. Instead, Chomsky proposes that there is indeed a richly structured organ that we may call the human mind which, without abandoning any of the rigour demanded by behaviourist structuralism, may be subjected to linguistic scrutiny.

To illustrate his position on the richness of the mind Chomsky poses a simple scientific riddle (Cook, 1985): how is it that native speakers come to know things about their language that could not have been learnt from the samples of speech that they have heard? How, for example, will the adult native speaker be (intuitively) able to distinguish between the **grammatical** sentence.

    (1) Is the book which is prescribed good?

and the **ungrammatical**

    (2) * Is the book which prescribed is good?

An adult speaker of English has the ability or grammatical competence, Chomsky would argue, to know that (1) is a possible sentence of English, while (2) is not. In other words, such an ideal speaker of the English language in some implicit sense knows that the 'is' that has been shifted to the beginning of a sentence comes out of the main clause ("The book ... is good") and has not been removed from the subordinate clause ("which is prescribed"). Now this 'knowledge' cannot possibly be derived from the speaker's experience of lingual stimuli, i.e. utterances he or she has heard before. Although speakers of English may conceivably have heard sentences such as

    (3) The book is good.
    (4) The book is a good one.
    (5) The prescribed book is good.
    (6) The book that is prescribed is good.
    (7) Is the book good?

and so on, none of these shows a violation of the syntactic rule, which can informally be stated as: "To change a statement into a question, move the auxiliary in the main clause to the initial position in the clause." It is only the **ungrammatical** concoction (2) that shows this violation, and it appears unlikely that the speaker would have heard this before. So the judgement of the native speaker regarding what are grammatical and ungrammatical sentences of the language cannot be based on experience, but on some property of the human mind:

> ... it makes sense to say ... that each person knows his or her language, that you and I know English for example, that this knowledge is in part shared among us and represented in our minds, ultimately in our brains, in structures that we can hope to characterize abstractly ... in terms of physical mechanisms. (Chomsky, 1982a: 5)

For the properties of mind that Chomsky wishes to investigate, he uses the term 'Universal Grammar'. This is a set of general principles of mind which determine the limits and parameters of any language, given the poorest of stimuli or 'triggers' to set such genetically determined 'growth' in motion (cf. Cook, 1985: 3; Chomsky, 1982a: 32ff.). In a word, Chomsky's approach is decidedly **mentalistic**, as opposed to the anti-mentalistic stance of the behaviourists. Moreover, Chomsky's position, in focussing on the possible structures of language, is overtly **rationalist**, whereas before linguistics had strong **empiricist** leanings.

Given the genetically inbuilt principles of mind that are called universal grammar, transformationalism claims also to have hit upon a way of explaining the acquisition of language by an individual. A child will, by listening to the language to which he or she is exposed, learn to fix the sentence order for that language as SVO (subject-verb-object) or SOV (subject-object-verb). In this way the environment, while being too 'poor' to provide sufficient evidence for learning a language without the aid of an inherent grammar, does provide positive evidence to fix the parameters of the language being learned in ways specified in principle by Universal Grammar.

By virtue of the native speaker's **competence** in the language, Chomsky claims that such a speaker is able to distinguish between possible (i.e. grammatical, acceptable) sentences of the language and impossible ones. This does not mean that all the sentences that native speakers will produce will be perfectly grammatical; quite the contrary. But to Chomsky's rationalist frame of mind such sentences may be disregarded (cf. Lyons, 1970: 39) since we are interested only in characterizing the **ideal** speaker's grammatical competence. Various slips and errors are (empirical) **performance** factors, i.e. characteristics of the utterances that actual (and not ideal) speakers produce when they are using the language.[1] Again, Chomsky is taking up a position that runs counter to the traditional, behaviourist view of linguistics, in that he assigns a crucial role to the **intuitions** of a native speaker. Where the behaviourist is interested primarily in the development and improvement of **techniques** of linguistic analysis, moreover, the transformationalist would see the proper task of linguistics as accounting for how well a particular grammar characterizes the intuitions and grammatical knowledge of a native speaker.

A **grammar** of a language in this sense means a theoretical instrument which should **generate** all and only the well-formed, grammatical sentences of a language. By generate (a technical term, which should not be confused with the actual production of utterances) Chomsky means: able to specify in abstract, formal terms. Here a further difference with behaviourist structuralism emerges: not only should such a grammar be *observationally* and *descriptively* adequate, but it must also strive to attain *explanatory* adequacy (cf. Radford, 1981: 25f.). This means that the grammar has to characterize a language in formal terms and principles that represent psychologically plausible mechanisms of mental computation.[2]

1. Chomsky himself points out the parallel in distinguishing between **competence** and **performance** and the Saussurean distinction of **langue** and **parole**. The different parts of each pair refer respectively to the **norm** side and the **factual** side of concrete language. Chomsky, like all rationalists, is interested mainly in the former.
2. In much of the psycholinguistic research that was stimulated by generativism, this notion was taken up quite concretely. For example,

The reception of Chomsky's theory, coming as it did in an environment that was entirely hostile to its basic tenets and assumptions, would not have been so overwhelmingly enthusiastic if it had not been backed up by substantial technical analyses that set out to realize the research goals of generative grammar. What follows is a very brief look at the technical details of Chomsky's theory.

As has been mentioned above, Chomsky's theories have, over the years, undergone developments and changes; his so-called Standard Theory has been succeeded first by an Extended Standard Theory, then by a modification of this known as Revised Extended Standard Theory or REST, several other modifications, and, finally, Minimalist theory. All along, though, right up to the very latest developments, the organization of his grammar has been (either implicitly or explicitly) **modular**, i.e. it is so organized that lingual phenomena are treated in separate components of the theory. Thus syntax, semantics and phonology are autonomous components. What changes from one theory to the next may be various interpretations of what should be treated under each component, but the essential modular approach has remained (cf. Radford, 1981: 12f.). One reason for adopting such an approach[3] is that problems of theoretical explanation occurring in one component or module are in a sense localized. If such problems can be solved by simply making adjustments

various so-called 'click'-experiments were set up to test the psychological reality, to native speakers, of theoretically distinguishable syntactic units. Subjects were asked to listen for the 'click' sound that had been inserted somewhere on the sound-track of an uttered sentence, and to mark the position of the 'click' on a transcribed version in front of them. Even though the click was displaced, in other words not positioned on a major phrasal or clause boundary, the subjects tended to hear it on the boundary! (cf. Clark & Clark, 1977: 53f.).

3. And there may be many reasons for adopting quite the opposite approach, hence much of the criticism of Chomskyan linguistics especially from the side of the so-called 'functionalist' perspective, which sees a rather stricter relationship between grammar and semantics. As will become clear below, the functionalist views grammar as a realization of different semantic choices, and therefore tries to explain the grammatical options chosen by appealing to semantic or functional explanations.

to one sub-part or component of the theory, there may be less serious implications for the others, and fewer modifications will eventually have to be made.

The Revised Extended Standard version of the theory (REST) posits two interacting systems in a **core grammar**, i.e. one of the limited number of grammars that a universal grammar would allow. There is, first, a sub-system of rules and, second, a sub-system of **principles** or conditions (cf. Waher, 1984: 5). For the purposes of this discussion, the sub-system of rules may be restricted to two components or modules:[4]

1. Lexicon
2. Syntax
    2.1 Base component (with output Deep or D-structures)
    2.2 Transformational component (with output S-structures)

The lexicon in a REST grammar is so organized that it contains all the words of the language being learned as entries that specify their meaning and syntactic features. The latter include the **subcategorization features** of a lexical item (Waher, 1984: 7). For example, the verb 'put' would have, as part of its subcategorization features, the specification

(8) + [_ NP - PP]

which means that it can occur only in the syntactic environment of a Noun Phrase followed by a Prepositional Phrase. This is evident when we look at

(9) The lecturer will put the books on the shelf

where 'put' is immediately followed by an NP (the books), which in its turn is followed immediately by a PP, and in that order, and when we consider the ungrammaticality of

---

4. There are more, but these are omitted since they are not crucial to the exposition. For example, S-structures form the input into a phonological component, with output surface structures.

(10) * The lecturer will put the books

as well as the ungrammaticality of

(11) * The lecturer will put

In examples (9), (10) and (11), it is clear that we have evidence for the lingual positioning of 'put' in line with the subcategorization rule (8). But is this enough evidence for adopting such a rule? Consider that there may be a problem in this specification of the subcategorization features of the verb 'put' in certain kinds of question in English,[5] if one considers that these features will wrongly predict that the following are impossible (ungrammatical) sentences of English:

(12) a. *Which books* will the lecturer put on the shelf?
    b. *Which books* does he say he will put on the shelf?

In (12) 'put' is followed in each case not by an NP, but by a PP: *on the shelf.* Before one rejects the subcategorization of 'put' as a verb that can occur only in the environment of an NP followed by a PP, one needs to consider that in other questions, specifically **echo-questions**, the feature (8) correctly predicts the grammaticality of

(13) The lecturer will put *which books* on the shelf?

and

(14) He said he would put *which books* on the shelf?

where both have the NP (*which books*) in its proper subcategorized position. Surely, in an approach that strives to achieve the greatest possible **generality**, one would prefer to have one set of subcategorization features over many. So Chomsky proposes

5. The subsequent argument will follow roughly that of Radford, 1981: chapter 5.

this solution: let us assume that there are (at least) two levels of structure, D-structure and S-structure. Then, at the underlying or deep level of structure, a sentence generated by the **base** component of the grammar would have the *wh*-element in its proper position according to subcategorization rules. What we need, subsequently, is a very simple (and eventually extremely general) **transformational** rule that would change this D-structure into an S-structure such as those (non-echo) questions that have *wh*-elements in preposed position. So from the underlying or D-structure

(15) The lecturer will put *which books* on the shelf?

we can, by moving the *wh*-element to the front (and by inverting the auxiliary and the subject noun phrase), get the S-structure

(16) *Which books* will the lecturer put on the shelf?

Movement rules are different from generative rules: they are rules not for explicating the form of sentences, but for **changing** or transforming them. As one early commentator on transformational-generative grammar, Gleason (1961: 172) had remarked, transformationalism treats "the structural relations of a pair of constructions ... as though it were a process." In terms of the distinctions introduced in the introduction, the spatial analogies within the lingual, that give content to notions of lingual sequence and position, are in transformationalist thinking made dynamic by introducing a set of kinematic analogies into the conceptualisation of structural lingual phenomena. This allows us to think about moving structural elements (such as the *wh*-element in the preceding examples) out of one sequential arrangement and into different lingual positions from their initially conceived place.

What, though, has been gained by introducing two levels of structure and a transformation rule? First, we now have an explanation for why the initial *wh*-elements in non-echo questions seem to act just like NP's occurring at some more **abstract** level, i.e. in exactly the position they would have in *wh*-echo questions such as (15); hence the position vacated by the *wh*-element leaves behind a **trace** as in the space marked _ in (17), thus satisfying subcategorization rules:

(17) Which books will the lecturer put $_{NP}$ [_] on the shelf?

Second, we no longer need to treat echo and non-echo questions differently in respect of syntactic structure, since both, at some underlying level, have exactly the same structure, and we have thus gained in terms of sought-after generality.

This ability of transformational grammar to treat apparently different phenomena in the same way syntactically is one of the major achievements of the theory. We have, in very broad outline, touched on only part of what may be gained in the case of two kinds of (direct) question, but this treatment applies *mutatis mutandis* also to other types of question formation, including indirect questions. What is more, one can produce further arguments for the existence of *wh*-**movement** phenomena by looking, for example, at the so-called **transitive prepositions**:

(18) a. * They are moving towards
b. * They are moving towards to reconciliation
c.   They are moving towards reconciliation

From the possibility of (18c) and the impossibility of (18a) and (18b) the preposition *towards* may plausibly be subcategorized as

(19) + [_ NP]

i.e., it will occur immediately before an NP. We run into problems again in questions such as

(20) What are they moving towards?

(where there is no NP directly following the preposition) if we do not allow for the possibility that (20) may be the output or S-structure of a D-structure along the lines of

(21) They are moving towards $_{NP}$ [*what*]?

which satisfies the subcategorization rule (19), viz. that the preposition *towards* has to occur in a lingual position before a noun phrase.

Nor should one consider only subcategorization arguments to include a transformational component in a generative grammar. Transformationalists argue that grammatical agreement phenomena also point to the same solution. Compare for example the grammaticality of

(22) These are the books which the lecturer said were on the shelf

with the ungrammaticality of

(23) * These are the books which the lecturer said was on the shelf

The ungrammaticality of (23) is accounted for if we allow for an empty NP in (22) that is plural in number (like *which*):

(24) These are the books which the lecturer said $_{NP}$ [e] were on the shelf

since NP [e] can at S-level be interpreted as the subject NP of the verb 'were' in (24), which, at some underlying level, had been subject to a rule of grammatical subject-verb agreement.

Or we could take an argument from contraction facts: why is it impossible to contract *he* and *has* to *he's* in (25), i.e. why does the language allow only for the grammaticality of (26)?

(25) * the books which he's on his shelf

(26)   the books which he has on his shelf

If we assume that before a constituent 'missing' at S-level as a result of the operation of a transformational rule on the output of structures at a deeper level, no contraction is possible, we have one possible explanation (there are others, too) for the ungrammaticality of (25), the S-structure of which may include a 'gap' to show that a constituent had been removed, as in

(27) the books which he has [_] on his shelf

If one now considers that the **wh-movement** rule does not move only NP's, but also PP's, AP's and AdvP's, cf.

(28)   a. *To whom* has he given the books PP [e]?
     b. *How strong* is it $_{AP}$ [e]?
     c. *How quickly* did you say he read it $_{AdvP}$ [e]?

the account appears to be more general still.6

What one has, in sum, are some highly abstract and at the same time very general treatments of phenomena that in most other analyses would receive disparate treatment. This is probably one of the most fascinating aspects of transformational-generative grammar, and explains some of its huge influence on linguistic theory.

Systemic/functional grammar

This school of linguistic analysis is today most closely associated with the name of Halliday, though its roots go back a long way in the history of English linguistics to scholars like Firth and Malinowski. Firth, who held the first chair of general linguistics in Britain, and his anthropologist friend, Malinowski, held the view that language can never be understood if it is isolated from the social contexts in which it is used (cf. Butler,

6. It can also be shown to apply to non-wh elements, such as NP's, in, for example, the formation of the passive (cf. Waher, 1984: 17f.).

1985: 2ff.; Sampson, 1980: 224ff.). From them Halliday took over the idea of language as an essentially social phenomenon. It is interesting to note that, whatever other differences of approach there may be between them, this (British) school of functional linguistics, had, like the descriptivists in America, derived the first stimulus for its work from the side of anthropology.

There are some important contrasts between the work of Halliday and Chomsky. While Chomsky would claim that the study of language is part of psychology and, ultimately, of biology (cf. Chomsky, 1982a: 185ff.; 1982b: 30), Halliday's views tend to see it as part of sociology (Halliday, 1978: 39). Where Chomsky is interested in the individual's capacity for learning a language, Halliday, in the tradition of English linguistics, is much more concerned with practical matters, i.e. with the functions that language fulfils in a social community. Chomsky adopts what Halliday (1978: 10) calls an **intra-organism** perspective, where he would take an **inter-organism** one. Coming as he does from a scientific tradition where rigour is the watchword, Chomsky would insist on the **autonomy** of syntax, conceding only that if the grammatical system interacts with other systems, such interaction would be "more or less on the periphery" (Chomsky, 1982b: 115). Halliday, like all functionalists (see note 3, above), sees a much more fluid relationship between the different levels of linguistic analysis (Butler, 1985: 3). Central to his thought is the notion that the 'meaning' is encoded in the 'wording', or, in technical terminology, that each level of language contributes to the expression or realization of meaning, the highest stratum in the hierarchy:

> The relation between the semantics and the grammar is one of realization: the wording 'realizes', or encodes, the meaning. The wording, in turn, is 'realized by' sound or writing. (Halliday, 1985: Introduction, p. xx)

Halliday (1978: 128) thus distinguishes three levels or **strata** that constitute the linguistic system:

(a) Semantic (the meaning)

(b) Lexicogrammatical (the wording, i.e. syntax, morphology and lexis)

(c) Phonological (the sound)

At the semantic level, Halliday distinguishes three components:

(i) ideational (further subdivided into experiential and logical parts)

(ii) interpersonal

(iii) textual

Any realization of the 'meaning' in the 'wording', in other words any concrete instance of actual language use, will, according to Halliday, be a simultaneous encoding or expression of all three semantic components in the lexicogrammatical stratum. At the lexicogrammatical level we therefore find the meaning of language 'constructed' or realized in the **simultaneous** selection of options (cf. Butler, 1985: 48).

Here another fundamental difference between a functionalist perspective and the Chomskyan approach can be seen. In the latter, Halliday claims, language is viewed as a system of **forms** to which meaning is then attached, a claim which is true in respect of Bloomfield's work, and perhaps the Standard Theory of transformational-generative grammar. In Halliday's perspective, however, the opposite tack is taken: language is seen as a system of **meanings**, accompanied or expressed by the forms through which they are realized (Halliday, 1985: Introduction, p. xiv).

The systemic part of Hallidayan linguistics attempts to show what grammatical **choices** or **options** have been chosen in any particular instance of text by the speaker to realize his or her expressive goals. To characterize the following utterances (grammatical options) by a speaker (in this case a mother, speaking to a naughty child. (Butler, 1985: 61f.)

(29) a. I'll smack you

b. Daddy'll smack you

c. Your bottom will get smacked soon

d. I'll be very angry if you do that again

e. If you go on doing that Daddy'll get very cross with you

f. If you don't stop you'll have to come inside

Halliday draws up the following **system network**:

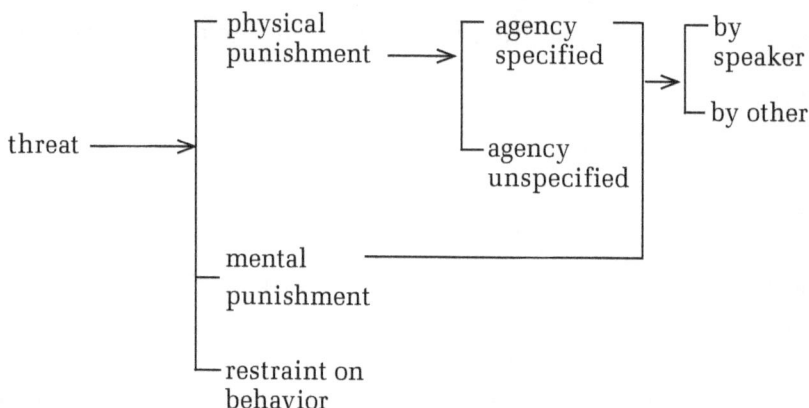

In a systemic analysis the emphasis is on language as a **system of choice**, and the system network above attempts to chart the possible choices that lie open to a speaker who wants to issue a threat.

Each of the examples given under (29a-f) above is a **realization** of one of the options in the system network. Language is viewed as 'meaning potential', actualized on the lexicogrammatical level.

Having briefly looked at the way that **questions** are treated in transformational-generative grammar, it is interesting to compare how systemic linguists deal with them. This sample **(corpus)** contains the different types of question in English:

(30) a. This is the one, is it? (tag, same polarity)

b. This is the one, isn't it? (tag, reverse polarity, rising intonation)

c. This is the one, isn't it? (tag, reverse polarity, falling intonation)

d. Is this the one? (yes/no, non-echo)

    e. This is the one? (yes/no, echo)
    f. Which one is it? (*wh-*, non-echo)
    g. This is which one? (*wh-*, echo)

Where the transformationalist would be interested in treating the analysis of such examples in as **general** a way as possible, the systemic linguist would see in this sample a realization of a grammatical network, or a set of grammatical options that are open to a speaker, and which may be characterized in the following way:

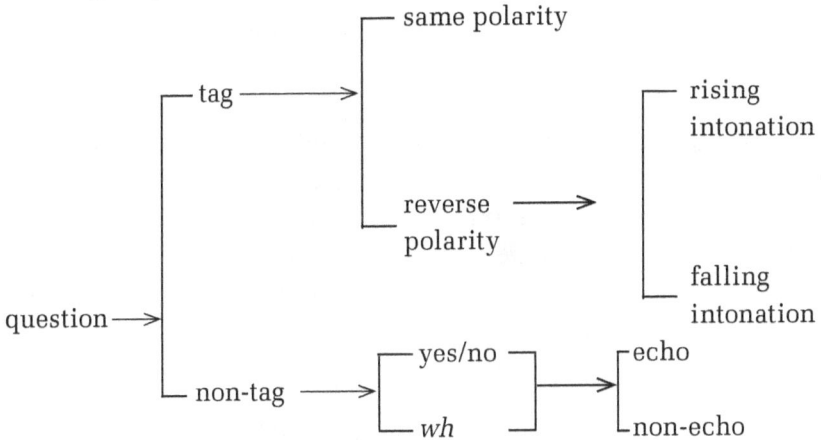

Such a presentation of grammatical options can be either less or more delicate, depending on the uses to which one would put the analysis. Moreover, there are other possible ways of presenting the same options, that would give theoretical expression to an even more general way of characterising questions:

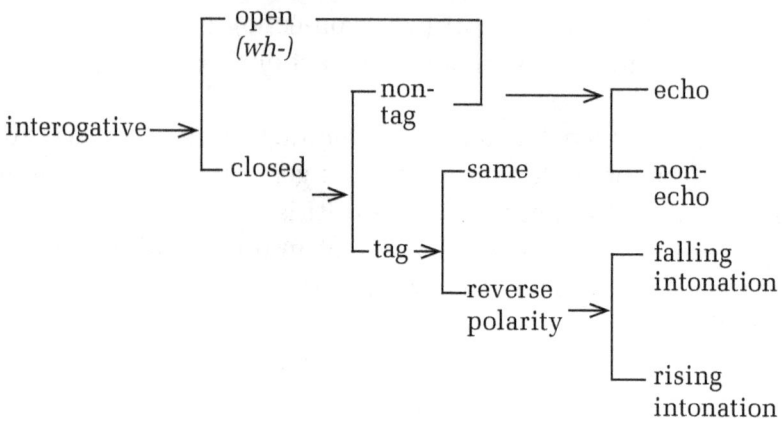

If the system network is presented in this way, it can be seen to fit into an even larger system network (cf. Berry, 1975: 166ff.) in the choice between **declarative** and **interrogative** sentences as options in the indicative mood. This system, in turn, fits into the higher system that regulates choices between **indicative** and **imperative** at the level of mood in English, thus:

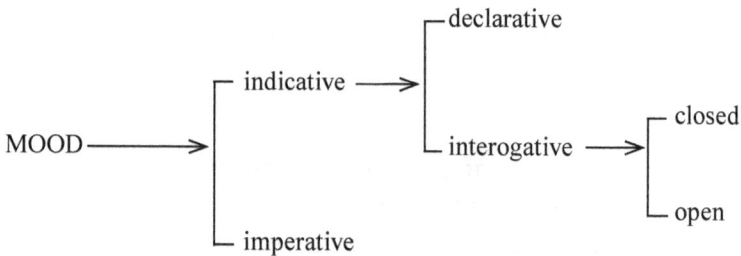

This has been one illustration of a single set of options open to a speaker at one level of realization. But Halliday stresses that in actually using a language, we make numerous choices or selections from several systems simultaneously. So, at the level of the (major) clause, we have, as speakers, not only choices of **mood**, but an additional set of choices on how, for example, the **theme** of such a clause may be realized (Butler, 1985: 52f.):

44

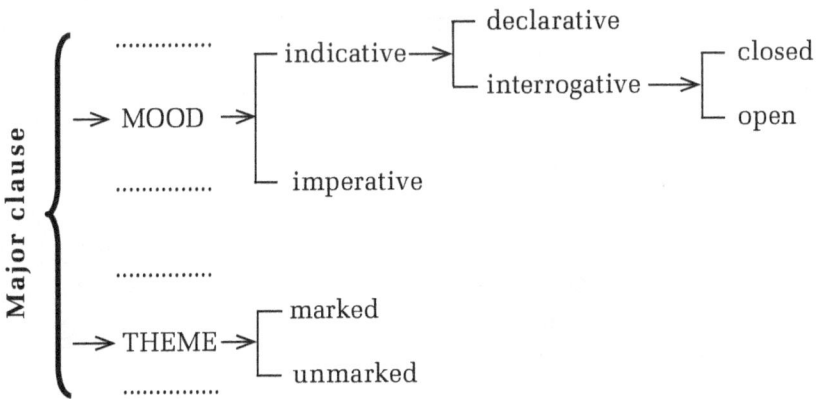

So, in (31) and (32), we have instances of major clauses in the indicative mood, realizing the declarative option in the latter, but differing in respect of **unmarked** and **marked** theme:

(31) Bruno gave Yogi a black eye
(32) What Bruno gave Yogi was a black eye

Halliday's notion of 'theme' ties in with a level of linguistic description that considers lingual phenomena 'beside the clause' (cf. Halliday, 1985: chapter 8), i.e. with a view to describing the clause as **message**, as a means of conveying what is lingually meaningful.

Where traditional or conventional approaches to grammar would take a **product** view, in other words focus only on the result (the lingual object that is produced by lingual subjects), Halliday is concerned, like many other approaches to the analysis of language today, with a **process** view. He therefore distinguishes a unit of linguistic description that may be called an **information unit** (Halliday, 1985: 274ff.). Even though the clause is not necessarily co-extensive with the information unit, it will be so in the unmarked case.

The information unit is organized so that there is an interplay in any instance of text between what is **given** and what is **new**. What is new at the level of the clause is given **prominence** in terms of its intonation contour (examples taken or adapted from Halliday, 1985: 275ff.):

(33) a. We're dealing with a nutcase here.
    b. Now nutcases need to have *love*.

where the prominence of *love* in (33b) marks the **end** of the new information the clause contains. Since *nutcase*, having been mentioned in (33a), is **given** in (33b), we may therefore assume that the information structure of the latter is as follows:

(34) $_{\text{Given}}$ [Now nutcases] $_{\text{New}}$ [need to have love]

Observe, once again, that in systemic functional grammar, as in other syntactic descriptions of English, the lingual **position** of elements within a lingual unit such as a clause or sentence – the sequentiality that we associate with spatial analogies in the lingual dimension of reality – is once again prominent. In the new lingual unit being dealt with here, that Halliday calls the information unit, the sequence or position of elements is always critically important to its lingual meaning-making. In (34) above, the lingual position of elements within the lingual information unit is a sequence of Given and New. This sequentiality is the usual (unmarked) position of given and new material in the information unit. But of course speakers have the option of putting new information first, as in

(35) *You* can go if you like, *I'm* not going

where the information structure is

(36) $_{\text{New}}$ [You] $_{\text{Given}}$ [can go if you like] $_{\text{New}}$ [I'm] $_{\text{Given}}$ [not going]

In (36) the information structure is **contrastive**, and therefore **marked**. The expectable lingual sequence (of Given followed by New) is inverted, so that the sequence, markedly, becomes New followed by Given.

Closely related to the information structure of a text is its **thematic structure**, already referred to above. 'Theme' Halliday defines as that which the speaker takes as his/her point of departure (Halliday, 1985: 278), what is being talked about.

Theme and **Rheme** structure does not necessarily coincide with Given and New, though: it does so only in the unmarked case. Theme + rheme is a speaker-oriented structure, while given + new is a listener-oriented device. In other words, the information structure tells the **listener** what is new (by making the end of the new element more prominent), while thematic structure is a conscious lingual choice on the part of the speaker to place the 'theme' he or she wishes to talk about in focus. There are several strategies for thematizing elements in English, some of which are exemplified in (37) to (40) below:

(37) a. *Alice* saw a mock turtle at the party
    b. *It was a mock turtle* that Alice saw at the party
                        ('It-clefting')

(38) a. He seems to get along with the neighbours,
       but *he* can't stand this one
    b. He seems to get along with the neighbours,
       but *this one* he can't stand
                       (Clefting)

(39) a. *I* am disgusted by this attitude
    b. *This attitude* disgusts me
                       (Quasi-passive)

(40) a. *He* has often helped Elaine
    b. *Elaine* has often been helped by him
                       (Passivization)

In the case of (37b) and (38b) above, 'theme' coincides not with 'given', but (markedly) with what is 'new'.

The **polyphonic** nature of an actual instance of language use is such that information structure and thematic structure are mapped onto each other to give a certain kind of (composite) **texture** to a text. To see how speakers achieve a certain kind of texture in a text, we may look at an example given by Halliday (1985: 279f.). In

> (41) A: Are you coming **back** into circulation?
> B: I didn't know I was **out**.
> A: I haven't **seen** you for ages.

we have, in A's last turn, a **marked** information structure

> (42) $_{New}$ [I haven't seen] $_{Given}$ [you for ages]

with the **new** information placed first. The thematic structure is, however, **unmarked**:

> (43) $_{Theme}$ [I] $_{Rheme}$ [haven't seen you for ages]

Why has Speaker A selected these choices? It is obvious from the rest of the dialogue that A needs to defend his first claim, and explain this in the light of B's complaint. He does so by choosing a composite lexicogrammatical structure, the texture of which, in terms of thematic and information structure, can **functionally** achieve this.

We shall be returning to other measures of texture; we have, however, seen sufficient examples of the selection, by speakers, of functionally important positions for elements in the clause, to know why this approach to the grammar of English is called **functional**. The deliberate, lingually meaningful **positioning** of functional elements in the clause is a further demonstration that an investigation of the reflection of the spatial dimension within the lingual is a linguistically worthwhile endeavour. Without this set of analogies, the kind of investigation of the formal sides of the language process that is conventionally undertaken by grammatical description, of whatever variety, would have been conceptually impossible.

The functional school of linguistic investigation, in emphasizing what speakers actually do with language, also provides an important bridge, for linguistic analysis, between such **formal** characterisations and **sociolinguistic** approaches to the study of the lingual dimension of reality. It is to the latter that we should direct our attention in order to get a more complete picture of what the rest of the linguistic encyclopaedia holds in store for us.

3 Socio-linguistic approaches: introduction

Beyond the sentence

The theoretical analysis of the lingual dimension of our experience in the previous chapter constitutes a close look at lingual forms. It dealt with different ways in which formal units of language can be analysed syntactically. Operating up to the level of the clause or sentence, it is called grammatical or syntactic analysis. This kind of linguistic analysis forms an important part of the linguistic encyclopedia. It accounts analytically for the ways in which syntactic sub-units such as words and phrases may be combined, sequentially, to make up clauses.

However, because in our pre-theoretical experience the concept of the "sentence" has become so firmly embedded, one can easily forget that this formal linguistic unit is really an abstraction, a theoretical concept that enables us to analyse lingual forms or structures. So, for example, when we look at the overall organization of a transformational-generative model of grammar (as in Radford, 1981: 390) we notice that the outputs of the various components (base, transformational, deletion, etc.) always concern structures, whether at D-level or S-level, that are more or less abstract characterizations of an equally abstract notion of the linguistic unit known as 'the sentence'. Similarly, the semantic component of such a grammar deals with the abstract notion of the 'logical form' of sentences, i.e. with the rules of sentence semantics. Phrased differently: transformational-generative grammar is irrevocably bound to (an abstract concept of) the sentence or clause; what it captures and characterizes, linguistically, is the sentence. Given this focus on abstract, general theory-formation in terms of those aspects of lingual phenomena that have - thus far - appeared to be susceptible to formalization, it is not strange that this kind of linguistic investigation has been labelled "theoretical" or "formal" linguistics.

But is this the only way of forming linguistic concepts? Does linguistic inquiry stop once it has reached the level of the sentence? Is the only sensible conclusion to be reached about a language like English that it is a set of well-formed sentences? The answer is clearly no, and this is why, alongside of the mainstream of theoretical linguistics there have over the last few decades been a number of studies that have tried to remedy this situation. As one linguist has rather jokingly pointed out:

> If we claim that natural language is a set of well-formed sentences, we might, by the same line of reasoning, maintain that sleep is a set of well-formed snores. For a grammar of sleep, we would set down some basic rules, such as
> $$SL = Sn1, Sn2, Sn3 \ldots Snn$$
> which allows us to "rewrite" sleep as an infinite set of snores (De Beaugrande, 1980: 15).

Despite all the objections of physiologists, De Beaugrande continues, we could simply go on to claim that such a "grammar of sleep" represents only the "competence" of an ideal sleeper, and that the actual process of sleeping does not concern us; the fits and starts, changes of snore in mid-breath, and so on, we might either comfortably ignore or consult our own intuitions about. By this rather bizarre argument De Beaugrande of course wishes to draw attention to the fact that actual language use, with all its fits and starts, fuzzy edges and inconsistencies, has systematically been disregarded by Chomskyan linguistics as a result of its pre-occupation with the linguistic (grammatical) competence of an ideal speaker. Instead, he says, we should acknowledge that

> People use natural language to manage situations and carry out plans. If they happen to produce and understand well-formed sentences along the way, their primary goals are quite different (De Beaugrande, 1980: 16).

Following more or less the same line of reasoning, one of the pioneers of sociolinguistic theory, Dell Hymes, in the mid-60's came to criticize Chomsky's views of language as being a "rather Garden of Eden view", and added that in this kind of linguistics, the

> ... controlling image is of an abstract, isolated individual, almost an unmotivated cognitive mechanism, not, except incidentally, a person in a social world (Hymes, 1971: 272).

This is an assessment which, no doubt, Chomsky himself would agree with. In a footnote in one of his major works, he states quite clearly that

> The knowledge of language attained by an individual in a real speech community is far more complex than under the idealization that we are considering, involving many styles of speech and possibly a range of interacting grammars (Chomsky, 1975: 232, note 4).

To be fair, we must also note that Chomsky at least in principle makes provision for other sets of rules beyond the rules of sentence grammar (cf. Chomsky, 1975: 104f.). He therefore does not deny the existence of sociolinguistics as a field of study; indeed, it is to him a part of linguistics, and moreover, a linguistics "that takes the idealization of ordinary linguistics one step closer to the complexity of reality" (Chomsky, 1979: 54). Nevertheless, Chomsky does not hesitate to add, almost in the same breath, that as a discipline sociolinguistics remains to him an obscure matter, and that he feels he has very little to contribute to it.

53

Beyond formal linguistics

What is to be done then if such a stalemate is reached? To quite a significant number of linguists the answer has been obvious: the security of the supposedly exact and rigorous road of "theoretical" or "formal" linguistics should be forsaken for the investigation of the "fuzzy edges" of actual language use. While formal linguistic theory may have something to say about some very general principles of the workings of language up to the level of the sentence, they have argued, there also has to be some way of theoretically coming to grips with language-in-use, i.e. with language in its social context. It is probably this realization, more than anything else, which has led to the development of sociolinguistic theory.

Of course, many linguistic studies over the years have had a social focus: traditionally, to take one example, the English language has had not only a grammar, but also a stylistics (cf. Matthews, 1981: 30). Moreover, there has always been the expectation in linguistics that its investigations will almost of necessity lead to the consideration of language in its social context. This, certainly, was the opinion of the arch-structuralist, Louis Hjelmslev, who already in 1943 had claimed that the self-imposed restrictive theoretical view in which only the system and constancy of language were investigated at the cost of the fluctuation and nuance of actual real-life language was only temporary, and that eventually the limited perspective had to give way:

> Linguistic theory is led by inner necessity to recognize not merely the linguistic system, ... but also man and human society behind language ... (Hjelmslev, 1963: 127)

These were prophetic words, foreshadowing the emergence of sociolinguistic enquiry. As one linguist (Searle, 1969: 17) has put it, a study purely of the formal features of language without eventually also considering the part played by these in speech acts "would be like a formal study of the currency and credit systems of economies without a study of the role of currency and credit in economic transactions."

An adjustment of focus

Sociolinguistic investigation therefore entails a shift in one's theoretical perspective, an adjustment of focus from a consideration of restrictive, highly general and abstract linguistic concepts and lingual units, to the specifying ideas that have to be employed to capture theoretically the links between the lingual and social dimensions of our experience.

If we account for this adjustment of focus in terms of the framework for linguistics analysis that I am employing here, it means that our theoretical gaze has to shift from a consideration of formal linguistic units to socially relevant lingual phenomena. From initially conceptualising linguistics as the investigation of *expression by means of signs,* we now have to consider how such expression deepens into *shared expression,* or *communication* (Weideman 2009).

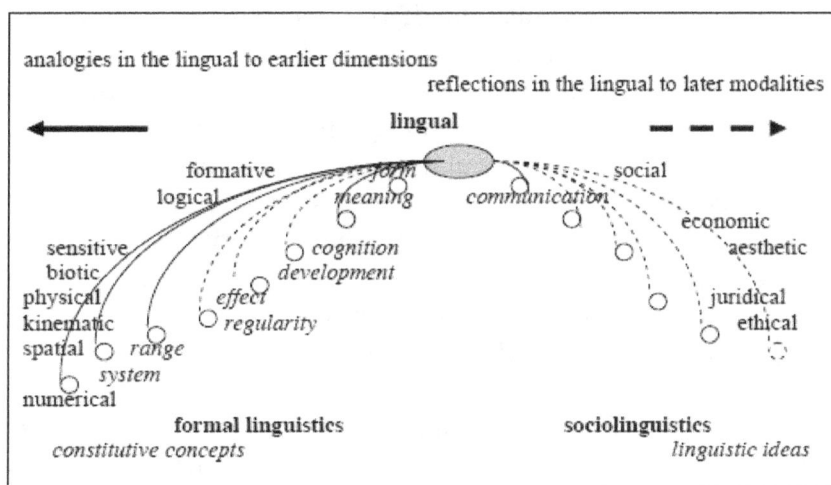

Figure 3.1: Formal linguistic concepts and sociolinguistic ideas

In Figure 3.1 above, we can see how the various analogies within the lingual dimension of experience have allowed us to conceptualise a number of basic linguistic concepts. There is the concept of lingual *system*, defined as a unity within a multiplicity of lingual norms and rules (the reflection of the numerical within the lingual), lingual position or *range* (the analogy of the spatial), lingual *regularity* (a reference within the lingual to the kinematic), and so forth.

However, when we do not restrict our theoretical investigation to these earlier reflections, but turn our analytical attention to enquire how the lingual dimension of experience opens up to reflect later modalities, a whole host of linguistic ideas, such as lingual *communication*, lingual *economy*, lingual *harmony*, lingual *justice*, lingual *care*, and lingual *trust* come into play. In what follows, we shall not have the time to deal with all of these, but only to consider theoretically some of the anticipations, within the lingual, of social life.

What is important for the current discussion is that in considering ideas generated by analogies within the lingual dimension referring to later dimensions, we have shifted our theoretical attention from constitutive linguistic concepts to regulative linguistic ideas. The distinction between **constitutive concept** and **regulative idea** derives from the references within the lingual dimension of experience that we are analysing to earlier aspects (those preceding the lingual) and to later aspects (those following the lingual). Those references that generate constitutive linguistic concepts are analogies to earlier modalities. The analogies to later dimensions within the lingual – also called anticipations, since they refer forward to later modalities - make possible our approximate conceptualisation of regulative linguistic ideas. The distinction is a crucial one for understanding, first, the difference in concept-formation between formal linguistics and sociolinguistics, and, second, the adjustment of theoretical focus that this entails.

This adjustment has been explained in different terms by various linguists: it has been called a shift from modular to interactional views of language (De Beaugrande & Dressler, 1981: 32), where "modular" refers to the fact that the various versions of transformational grammar seek to separate out the theoretical apparatus of such a grammar into a number of different modules (base component, transformational component, etc.) each with its own specific characteristics (Arnold & Bennett, 1982: 2ff.), the idea being that the modularity of the theory will allow problems to be localized (and solved) much more easily. This shift of focus may also be termed, with Habermas (1970), a transition from monological to intersubjective perspectives; or, if we prefer a somewhat less obscure characterisation, we may invoke the distinction that Halliday (1978: 10) makes between intra-organism and inter-organism views of language. From an intra-organism perspective we look at the language knowledge of an isolated (ideal, abstract) individual, i.e. at the internal mechanisms or make-up that makes possible the production and understanding of language in the individual. In the inter-organism perspective, on the other hand, language is viewed as the form or means of social interaction. Whatever the names are by which this shift in linguistic attention is characterized, it is clear that, in some way, "formal" theoretical and sociolinguistic approaches are complementary: each focuses on different facets of language. Just what the exact nature of such complementarity might be will only become clear later, but the main point to be made here is this: in reaction to the idealized constructs of theoretical linguistics, there has emerged a readiness to tackle the rather more complicated problem of analysing language as it is used in human interaction.

This readiness to grapple with the social dimensions of language goes a long way towards explaining the excitement that characterizes linguistic investigation today. The fascination of discovering not only very general principles of language at the level of the sentence, but also highly regular forms of organization in, for example, the apparently chaotic material of conversation, constitutes a good part of what makes linguistics a vibrant discipline.

We shall be dealing here with only a few of the major ideas and themes advanced in sociolinguistic investigation. The selection of ideas and themes is, like all selections, somewhat arbitrary, but those that are discussed here have been included mainly on the basis of their possible relevance to practical concerns with language, such as language teaching.

Before turning to some of the central themes in the chapters that follow, let us first take a look at three major sociolinguistic ideas: the idea of communicative competence, the idea of discourse types and the notion of "text".

Communicative competence

Although other scholars (e.g. Habermas, 1970) were, in the late 60's, developing similar ideas, Hymes's essay on communicative competence (Hymes, 1971) was probably the most influential, particularly among sociolinguists and applied linguists.

It is especially interesting to see how Hymes redefines Chomsky's distinction between (lingual) competence and performance. Rejecting the notion that "competence" can refer only to the grammatical *knowledge* of the speaker/listener, and that "performance" acts as a kind of residual category for factors such as *appropriateness* and *acceptability*, he goes on to develop a broader idea of what he calls a 'differential competence'.

Taking competence as a wide term for the capabilities of a person, Hymes argues that this underlying ability includes not only the knowledge of whether a stretch of language is grammatically possible (a notion roughly equivalent to Chomsky's concept of the intuition of a native speaker of the language in respect of the grammaticality or well-formedness of a sentence), but also the capacity to know whether such a stretch of language is acceptable and appropriate. There are many perfectly grammatical sentences of English - and we may think of many examples in current textbooks on grammar, such as

(1) This boy will speak very slowly to that girl.
(2) John gave the postman a parcel.
(3) Mary considers herself to have outwitted Paul.

– that may perhaps have been used to illustrate a profound point of grammar, but which are nonetheless neither acceptable (feasible) in certain contexts, nor even *lingually appropriate*, either on their own, or strung together:

(4) This boy will speak very very slowly to that girl.
John gave the postman a parcel. Mary considers herself to have outwitted John.

Indeed, stretches of language such as (1)-(3) and (4) would in most contexts be highly inappropriate, except perhaps as examples in a linguistics textbook.

According to Hymes, we have the knowledge or the competence to make such judgements of feasibility or acceptability as normal members of a lingual community. This is our communicative command or competence: an ability to use language in ways that are feasible and appropriate in different contexts. Moreover, this communicative competence is part of the general interactional competence that underlies our "performance" in social life, our interaction with others.

To sum up the differences between the theoretical linguistic concept of lingual competence and the sociolinguistic idea of communicative competence: the former explains judgements of the grammaticality of sentences made by ideal speakers in a homogeneous speech community, and is thus highly abstract and general; the latter concerns the capacity of a normal member of a community to judge whether (a stretch of) language is used not only grammatically, but also appropriately in contexts that are typically different. Though perhaps more difficult to conceptualise in formal terms, the idea of communicative competence is thus much more specific in its focus than the merely lingual competence that Chomsky sets out to characterise theoretically.

These two notions of competence, Chomsky's and Hymes's, are at the same time good illustrations of the difference between a constitutive linguistic concept and a regulative linguistic idea, a distinction that was introduced above as being critically important for understanding the difference between formal linguistics and sociolinguistics. Chomsky's concept remains firmly bound to the restrictive linguistic analysis that yields insight into constitutive linguistic concepts, while Hymes's sociolinguistic idea of communicative competence provides evidence of a disclosure of our theoretical view in a regulative idea that transcends formal concept-formation.

The sociolinguistic idea of a communicative command of language is a notion that attempts to clarify how a user is able to produce language appropriate to the situation. This idea naturally brings up the question of lingual context or, rather, the differentiated variety of lingual contexts that we as users of language, as lingual subjects, encounter from day to day, as well as the various types of discourse that are associated with different situations. How do we conceptualise these?

Types of discourse

Let us try to explain the idea of a variety of types of discourse that are appropriate in different contexts by starting with an example. If we take the utterance

(5) This is cute! "Bosal wants to lift the world"!

we might run into serious difficulties of understanding and interpretation if we do not share a number of assumptions with whosoever has uttered these two sentences, and, as we shall see subsequently, with the original author of the second. Utterance (5) would scarcely make any sense as an interpretable lingual object if the person (lingual subject) to whom it is addressed cannot see, or for some reason does not know, that the speaker is reading a newspaper at the time of uttering (5), or, further, that the speaker is commenting ("This is cute!") on the caption (*Bosal wants to lift the world*) of a report in a newspaper she is reading. For a lingual object such as (5) to become interpretable, we need to explore what communicative contexts lingual subjects share. We can therefore only come closer to a full understanding of the utterance if we also know that the caption "Bosal wants to lift the world" headed a report in the business news section of the newspaper and, furthermore, that the report in question deals with the success that an exhaust-pipe manufacturing company called Bosal had had in increasing its profits chiefly through the production of motor car jacks during the financial year that was being reported on.

This example wants to say, quite simply, that an utterance hardly makes any sense if it is either taken out of its context, or removed from the situation in which it occurred. And this is the case because language *an zich* - pure, ideal, abstract language - does not exist. In written or in spoken form, language is always used in a specified context, and in a typical situation.

The statement that language does not exist in a void or vacuum may at first glance look both obvious and trivial, yet developments in theoretical linguistics over the last quarter of a century that have tended to emphasize artificially restricted, presanatized data (Givon, 1979: 81), have made it necessary for linguists to be reminded of this fact once again. Of course, to be more specific, we must go on to say that language operates in various spheres or zones, and that the language used in these zones differs from one sphere to the next.

If one compares the language of poetry to that of academic discourse, or the at times long-winded legal language of an insurance policy with the terseness of an army telex message, one immediately realizes that there are distinct differences among the various types of language used in these typically different contexts. All of the following examples may have some communicative (i.e. social) intent, yet the realization of this by objective lingual means is typically different in each:

(6) My aspens dear, whose airy cages quelled,
    Quelled or quenched in leaves the leaping sun,
    Are felled, felled, are all felled...
                    (G.M. Hopkins)

(7) When Kant comes to the transcendental
    exposition of time, we would expect that he
    would attempt to prove that time as an a priori

intuition is a necessary and sufficient
condition for making synthetic a priori
judgements in arithmetic.
                    (Hartnack, 1968: 25)

(8) It is hereby declared and agreed that should a
    tenant of the Insured in the within insured
    building do or omit to do, without the
    knowledge or consent of the Insured,
    anything which would vitiate the within policy
    conditions and/or warranties, section 7 of
    this policy will not be held to be void on
    that account provided that the Insured shall
    notify to the Company the happening .....

(9) BT UNCLASS INF/161 JUL 75

    1. G/TRG 6/37 INF 7526 OVER G/TRG/6/37 441R
    2. YOUR TRG/269 JUL 75 REFERS
    3. ITO THE AMNEDED ATI A COMDS TO
    INFORM CF UNITS CONCERNED OF
    PARA 6 OF 2 ABOVE

Formally, linguistics has tried to grasp these differences
in that branch of language study that is known as stylistics. A
stylistic analysis might, for instance, reveal that in (6)-(9) there
are differences on both the lexical and syntactic levels. So one
would find words and phrases like "transcendental", "a priori",
"necessary and sufficient" and "synthetic ... judgements" in
academic discourse, but certainly not the suggestive "airy cages",
"quenched in leaves" and "the leaping sun" of Hopkins's poems.
Likewise, the formulaic "declared and agreed", "the within
insured building" and "shall notify to the company" in (8) that
are so typical of the insurance policy, will not be found in the
rather cryptic syntax of the army telex message of (9), where
strange combinations like "G/TRG/6/37 INF 7526" may occur
side by side with highly specific abbreviations like "ITO" and

"ATI" (meaning respectively: "in terms of" and "Army Training Instructions"). In the latter case, the urgency and speed with which messages like (9) are sent may cause "errors" of some sort: note, for example, "AMNEDED" for "amended", "A COMDS" (probably meaning only "commands" - there seems to be no use for "A") and the missing stroke in the first "G/TRG 6/37" of the first paragraph. Again, we would not expect such slips and errors in the careful wording of a stretch of language such as (8).

All these formal, stylistic differences ask for some form of explanation, however. How does it come about, we may ask, that such differences exist? One possible explanation is that, from a sociolinguistic point of view, such lingual variation stems from the differing (social) purposes to which language is put; that these formally identifiable varieties of language are related to socially variable types of discourse. In this way earlier studies in English stylistics (e.g. Crystal & Davy, 1969) have paved the way for the investigation not only of written texts (as in (6)-(9), above), but also for the sociolinguistic analysis of different kinds of speech.

Although much of the sociolinguistic investigation of different types of discourse is still in its infancy, we do already know some fascinating things about this variety. We know, for instance, that our intuitions about the fact that things are not said the same way when a superior addresses an inferior, and vice versa, are born out by empirical tests. One very interesting piece of research (Kemper & Thissen, 1981) has noted that only superiors are allowed by the rules of talk to use direct requests, such as

(10) Rake the leaves

as well as rather indirect ones, such as

(11) I think the leaves need to be raked.

Subordinates, on the other hand, are restricted, in addressing a superior, to indirect requests like (11). Moreover, should a subordinate, in violation of the sociolingual rules of talk, make the wrong choice and use an inappropriate (in this case: direct) form of request in addressing a superior, it is very likely that this inappropriate form will be accurately remembered by the superior! The relevance of the results of this research to second and foreign language learning is obvious: teachers cannot simply teach their non-English speaking pupils one pure form of requesting in English, for there are various forms available that are appropriate to different types of discourse; ideally, teaching "requests" in English should, at the very least, grade the different forms available according to varying degrees of politeness, and devise pedagogical ways of practising these.

Similarly, talking is different in a context where there is an authority relationship (with super- and subordination of speakers) from the face to face conversational encounters between social equals. Also, there is variation in talk between people who have relatively durable relationships (whether as equals or as superiors and subordinates) and between those who do not. We do not talk to strangers the same way as we would to our children/parents. Everything we know in this regard emphasizes, but now from a sociolinguistic point of view, what stylisticians have been telling linguists all along:

> When we talk about "a language" - in our case, "the English language" - we must not be misled into thinking that the label should in some way refer to a readily identifiable object in reality, which we can isolate and examine in a classroom as we might a test-tube mixture ..... there is no such object. The label "the English language" is in fact only a shorthand way of referring to something which is not, as the name may seem to imply, a single homogeneous phenomenon at all, but rather a complex of many different "varieties" of language in use in all kinds of situation ... (Crystal and Davy, 1969: 3).

Contrary, too, to what prescriptive grammarians have said about "good" or "correct" English, sociolinguistic enquiry must maintain that there is no one correct form of English for all occasions, but many different appropriate forms. And it is our sociolingual, communicative competence that enables us to make the delicate choices according to (sociolingual) norms of appropriateness, efficiency, and so forth. We know which "register" of language (Halliday, 1978: 110f.) to expect and to use in each different type of discourse we participate in as lingual subjects. Gossiping is not the same kind of talk as asking information from a stranger, cajoling children or giving a lecture, and we somehow manage to switch from the one register of language to the other without crashing our lingual gears.

To sum up: the different types of discourse seem to vary along different axes: talk in an **institutional** relationship (which has both an authority structure and a durable unitary character independent of changes in the individual membership of the relation) is different from that in a **communal** relationship (which has either an authority structure or a unitary character, but not both), and both of these types of discourse are typically different from the talk we expect in an **associational** relationship between equals (such as friendship) which possesses neither an authority structure nor a unitary character. Furthermore, the language used in any type of discourse is different from that of another type, because the kind of social action that characterizes a relationship may vary: there are typically academic relationships (as between lecturers and students) and typically economic ones (as between shopkeeper and client), to give but two examples. In each of these relationships these typical differences will show up in the language that is used.

"Text" as linguistic unit

The third sociolinguistic idea to be discussed here is that of **text** as linguistic unit. It is generally agreed today that this unit may refer to either the written or spoken forms of language. Where linguistic theory has always had to employ some notion of lingual norms (conditions for language) and lingual facts (actual instances of language that are subject to such conditions) - and here we may think of distinctions such as those between *langue* and *parole* (de Saussure) and competence and performance

(Chomsky) - sociolinguistics utilizes the idea of (normative) types of discourse that determine the nature of factual texts.

"Text" is therefore the linguistic form of social interaction (Halliday, 1978: 122). Where theoretical linguistics needs formal linguistic units such as the word, phrase, clause and sentence, sociolinguistics is in need of lingual units such as "speech act", "move", "exchange" and "text", that take into account the interactive, social meaning and use of language. This is why Halliday (1978: 139f.) says:

> The essential feature of text ... is that it is interaction. The exchange of meanings is an interactive process, and text is the means of exchange: in order for the meanings which constitute the social system to be exchanged between members they must first be represented in some exchangeable symbolic form, and the most accessible of the available forms is language. So the meanings are encoded in (and through) the semantic system, and given the form of text.

In sociolinguistic terms, lingual expression deepens into exchangeable, shared expression, into communication. Texts are, as Halliday points out, the lingual objects that are the forms or units in which such lingual sharing takes place.

It was again Hjelmslev, the Danish linguist, who foresaw the study of texts as the objects of linguistic inquiry (Hjelmslev, 1963: 16), and it is to a consideration of text linguistics that we shall subsequently turn.

Sociolinguistic approaches: introduction

4 Text linguistics

L ike any other scientific discipline, linguistics deals with objects or sets of objects that are considered to be theoretically relevant to its field. In formal linguistics, we need to know what a word or lexical item is, what a phoneme is, what a clause or sentence is, and so forth. Various definitions for these have been discussed and advanced since the inception of modern linguistics, and various formal criteria have been proposed for determining lingual units, such as the word or lexeme, and their constituents. Not all the formal linguistic criteria employed to define lingual objects are straightforward or uncontested. Sometimes we need to go through various sets of fairly sophisticated analytical tests to make these determinations. For example, in order to delimit clauses, we may have to look at the distribution, co-ordination, omission, intrusion, etc. of the phrasal categories contained in the sentence (cf. Radford, 1981: 68f.).

When linguistics ventures beyond the sentence, however, it becomes increasingly difficult not only to determine what the units of linguistic analysis are, but also to conceptualize how these units can be defined. In short: while formal linguistics can operate conceptually in terms of formally defined units, sociolinguistic analysis needs linguistic ideas to approximate the units of linguistic analysis that fall within its purview.

One such lingual unit operative beyond the level of the sentence, as we have noted in the previous chapter, is that of text. As a unit of linguistic analysis it goes back at least to the work of the structuralist Hjelmslev (1963), who already in 1943 had recognized its usefulness as concept. Such acknowledgement, however, is only the beginning of the intellectual task to delimit, define and conceptualize this notion. So, for example, Halliday (1978: 137ff.) stresses the "essential indeterminacy" of the idea of text; whereas clauses or sentences are relatively well-defined entities, with (formally) specifiable beginnings and endings, these are less easily identifiable in 'texts': a text is a "seamless unit", according to Halliday. Whether this is indeed so is one of the problems that will be addressed in what follows.

Given the acknowledgement of text as linguistic unit, however, there are certain criteria that a text must meet in order to be a text, i.e. criteria to distinguish **text** from **non-text**.

Standards of textuality

Most text linguists seem to agree, firstly, that text is the objective linguistic form of social interaction, a communicative occurrence (Halliday, 1978: 122; De Beaugrande & Dressler, 1981: 3). This means that a text may be either spoken, written or gestural in form (or a combination of these). It follows, therefore, that what is non-text is also non-communicative lingual expression. It is hard to find instances of non-text, but the following example of talk between a doctor and a psychiatric patient (Coulthard, 1985: 6) comes very close to it:

(1) A: What is your name?
   B: Well, let's say you might have thought you had something from before, but you haven't got it anymore.
   A: I'm going to call you Dean.

De Beaugrande & Dressler (1981) discuss several standards of textuality, i.e. criteria that a text must fulfil in order to be a text.

They are

(a) cohesion
(b) coherence
$\left.\right\}$ objective, text-centred criteria

(c) intentionality
(d) acceptability
(e) informativity
(f) situationality
(g) inter-textuality
$\left.\right\}$ subjective, user-centred criteria

We shall be concerned mostly with the first two criteria. Let us therefore first briefly review the others.

If a text is always to be communicative, as our definition says, then it follows that it must be **informative** too. Platitudes, clichés, and statements of what is boringly obvious, compare

(2) The earth revolves around the sun.
(3) Western values must be preserved.
(4) This government has always protected the right to self-determination.

all come very close to a violation of this norm of textuality: they are either devoid of any content, trite, or boring.

A text may also be deemed **acceptable** or **unacceptable**. B's reply in the following is obviously unacceptable to the receiver A, as his response shows:

(5) A: Good morning!
B: It certainly isn't.
A: I beg your pardon?

Acceptability here is simply the **social** acceptability of a lingual utterance, and such acceptability depends on the normative evaluation of the objective lingual text by a lingual subject other than the producer of that text, i.e. on the judgement of a hearer/reader. There is thus a socially differentiated role for lingual subjects when expression deepens into communication:

they can be, as in this instance, either hearers, or speakers (or, in other instances, readers and writers).

The **intentionality** of a text, on the other hand, concerns not the hearer or reader's, but the producer's attitude to the text: if the producer of a text strives to create a text that is informative, acceptable, and so on, the product may be slightly incoherent, shoddy or grammatically awkward, yet still reflect the intention, goal or plan of the speaker in producing it; and if this intention is successfully understood by the addressee, the text as a whole might nonetheless succeed. As examples one may think here of the stops and starts, changes of lingual direction in mid-sentence, and so forth, that are so frequent in conversation. Thus K's utterance in (6)

> (6) K: You wanna hear muh - eh my sister told me a story
> last night.
> R: I don't wanna hear it.
> (Levinson, 1983: 323)

might still succeed as a text, as R's reply would indicate, on account of K's ability, in spite of his grammatical change of direction, to convey to R his intention of telling a joke.

The **situationality** and **inter-textuality** of texts are closely related to the coherence of a text. The sign (De Beaugrande & Dressler, 1981: 1)

> (7) SLOW
> CHILDREN
> AT PLAY

can, for example, be a highly ambiguous instance of text if it is not interpreted against the background of the situation of its occurrence (as a sign next to a public road, not a socially inappropriate one on, say, the door of a room in a school for handicapped children) or knowledge of the terseness of the class/kind of text it belongs to (road sign), i.e. its **inter-textuality**, or the inferences through which we make sense of a text (its coherence).

Not all texts are required to be unambiguous, however. Poetry can be and often is intentionally ambiguous, and our expectations of a poetic text are defined by its situationality, inter-textuality, and the accessibility of its underlying sense(s), i.e. the inferences we might make about it as a whole.

Of particular importance to text linguistics, however, are the standards of **coherence** and **cohesion**, for these, perhaps more than any of the other criteria, define the wholeness or unity of a text. Both deal with the continuity or connectedness of texts, but cohesion is a term that is usually reserved for **verbally explicit** connectedness, while coherence is used to indicate a **non-verbally explicit** connectedness.

Again, it is hard to find instances of texts that are not simultaneously cohesive and coherent. (8) is an instance of cohesive text, since there is a verbally explicit continuity between one part of it and another:

(8) The new rules come into effect on January 1. They
     must be replaced within 40 sitting days of Parliament.
                   (*The Guardian*, 4 January 1983)

"They" in the second sentence explicitly marks a connection of this sentence with the first, since it refers back to "the new rules." In (9), however, there is no such verbally explicit connectedness:

(9) Father: Here it comes!
    Class members: Breathe! Bear down!

Yet the continuity or wholeness of (9), even though it lacks cohesion in the technical sense, is guaranteed by the continuity of sense(s) that it displays, its **coherence**. It is, first, a cartoon dialogue, the continuity of which depends on our **shared knowledge** of what happens during childbirth. The cartoon, which pokes fun at the rather sophisticated rituals that rich Westerners go through during such events, depicts the critical moments of an actual birth occurring right in the middle of a pre-natal exercise class, where it is least expected. The almost primitive chant of the class members further stresses the ironic aspects of the situation. The **coherence** of a text therefore depends not on verbally explicit, grammatical links between sentences, but on our shared knowledge of the world and the texts that reflect this.

An often-cited instance of text that possesses coherence, but not cohesion, is (10):

(10) A: Can you go to Edinburgh tomorrow?
      B: BEA pilots are on strike.

Whether this is indeed so is, however, problematic. We could also interpret (10) as cohesive, if we suppose that B's reply might entail ellipsis, which, as we shall see below, is an instance of one kind of cohesion:

(11) A: Can you go to Edinburgh tomorrow?
      B: [*sc.*(You jolly well know that) (I can't ((*sc.* go
         to Edinburgh tomorrow)) because)] BEA pilots
         are on strike.

But this example serves to illustrate the difficulty of distinguishing between cohesion and coherence, and of course does not do away with the distinction as such; as has been pointed out, it is difficult to find examples of texts that are not simultaneously cohesive and coherent.

Nevertheless, there are other problems connected with the distinction between cohesion and coherence, and to see what these are, let us examine first the cohesive relations within one kind of text.

Types of cohesion[1]

Various types of cohesion are to be found in both spoken and written texts (cf. Halliday & Hasan, 1976). There is cataphoric (forward) **reference**, where a word or phrase in one clause refers

1. For the greater part of the subsequent analysis, see Weideman (1984).

forward to another, in a subsequent phrase; there is anaphoric (backward) reference, where a phrase or word in a subsequent phrase refers back to one in an earlier clause. Then there is a kind of verbally explicit connectedness that is known as **substitution**, where a word like "so" or "such" is substituted for a word or phrase encountered earlier. This kind of cohesion is linked closely with **ellipsis**, where, as in (11) above, certain words or phrases are "understood" to be present (although they have been omitted) in order to interpret the text. The other two types, **conjunction** and **lexical cohesion**, are self-explanatory.

Let us look at instances of these different types of cohesion in an actual text. The text that has been chosen to illustrate these is the following sonnet:

(12) ON HIS BLINDNESS (a)

When I consider how my light is spent
Ere half my days in this dark world and wide,
And that one talent which is death to hide
Lodged with me useless, though my soul more bent
To serve therewith my Maker, and present
My true account, lest he returning chide,
'Doth God exact day-labour, light denied?'
I fondly ask (b). But Patience, to prevent
That murmur, soon replies, 'God doth not need
Either man's work, or his own gifts (c). Who best
Bear his mild yoke, they serve him best (d). His state
Is kingly: thousands at his bidding speed,
And post o'er land and ocean without rest (e(i));
They also serve who only stand and wait' (e(ii)).

John Milton (f)

We find instances here of both kinds of **reference**: cataphoric (forward) and anaphoric (backward). So the word "his" in (12a) refers forward to "I" in sentence (12b) and "John Milton" in (12f). Both are examples of cataphoric reference. There are quite a few anaphoric references, the most obvious being the several uses of "I", "my", and "me" in sentence (12b) to "his" in (12a). This kind of reference can in turn be either personal, as in the examples given above, demonstrative, as in "that (murmur)" in sentence (12c), which refers back to the rebellious[2] question in sentence (12b), or comparative (cf. Halliday & Hasan, 1976: 31ff.), of which "only (stand)" in sentence (12e(ii)) might be a possible instance because it refers back to "(post) ... without rest" in sentence (12e(i)) and 'serve' in sentence (12d).[3]

There seem to be no examples in (12) of **substitution**, as in (13) below. In (13), the specific kind of substitution is clausal substitution, since "so" replaces and is an abbreviated substitute for all of which follows "that Mr Young's ..."

> (13) ... it seemed that Mr Young's "I" was merely shorthand for "the Commission." Perhaps that will be so, but when this £10 millions scheme ...
>
> (*The Guardian*, 4 January 1983)

Within the cohesive category of **substitution**, there are again various sub-types, with nominal, verbal and clausal substitution being the major subdivisions (Halliday & Hasan, 1976: chapter 3) that present systemic choices to producers of text.

Apart from its lack of examples of substitution, our example text (12) also has no instances of **ellipsis**, as in

> (14) Christopher Price: "You seem to be a passionate advocate of mixed ability teaching?"
> David Young ...   "Yes."
>
> (*The Guardian*, 4 January 1983)

where "Yes" should be read as "Yes, I am a passionate advocate, etc." Considered systemically, ellipsis is merely a particular

---

2. "Fondly" in sentence (12b) means "foolishly."

3. A systemic representation of the options in the reference system would thus be

reference ——— [anaphoric ／ [personal
                                demonstrative
                                comparative
               cataphoric

kind of substitution, namely substitution by zero (cf. Halliday & Hasan, 1976: 89, 143, 317; also Matthews, 1981: 38ff.). On the other hand, there are in (12) a number of instances of lexical cohesion and conjunction, the remaining two types of cohesive relation discussed by Halliday and Hasan (1976) in *Cohesion in English.*

Let us look first at **conjunction** (Halliday & Hasan, 1976: chapter 5; cf. too 320ff.). "But" in (12c) is the explicit indicator of a conjunctive relation between (12b) and (12c). It is clear that these two sentences, containing the poet's rebellious question and the reply of Patience, form a sequence that achieves a "relatedness beyond that which may otherwise obtain between related utterances", a relatedness that according to Schegloff and Sacks (1973: 295f.) exhibits the operation of one type of typology of sequence, that of question and answer.[4] Less clear, however, is the cohesive status of items such as "soon" in (12c) and the colon and "..;... also" in sentence (12e(i)). "Soon" might be classified as a complex temporal conjunctive (cf. Halliday & Hasan, 1976: 337), co-operating with "But", while the colon may have any of several of the meanings of conjunctive items discussed by Halliday and Hasan, most probably being a causal conjunction between the first and second clauses of the sentence. It is also possible to regard "..;... also" as a simple additive conjunction.

Indicating **lexical cohesion** (Halliday & Hasan, 1976: chapter 6) in (12) is also more problematic than is to be expected. It seems that neither reiteration, which comprises the repetition of a lexical item or synonym of some kind, nor collocation, i.e. the mutual expectancy between co-occurring words, can in all cases be identified in (12) without reference to the typical features of poetic language. The typifying characteristic of poetic language is that it is highly allusive in reference (cf. Seerveld, 1980: 128) and typically employs such unusual collocations.

It is easy to see that "blindness" in the title is a cataphoric

---

4. (12b) and (12c) satisfy all three conditions for adjacency pairs that exhibit a typology of sequence, being (a) two utterances long, (b) adjacent and (c) produced by different speakers (Schegloff & Sacks, 1973: 295; cf. too chapter 6, below).

reference to "light denied" and could collocate also with "dark" in (12b), while 'murmur' has a reiterative quality. Reiteration, as a type of lexical cohesion, usually occurs with "the" or a demonstrative, as in "that murmur" in (12c). Since 'murmur' in turn presupposes the foolish question at the end of (12b), we have a double cohesive tie in this instance. Another instance of lexical cohesion can be found in "replies" in (12c), which is the expected collocational item after "ask" in (12b). Similarly, the lexically reiterative chains of "Maker", "he", "God" (all in 12b), "God", "his" (12c), and of "serve" (12b), "serve" (12d), "speed", "post" and "serve" (12e) present little difficulty. But it is perhaps less easy to see that "work" in (12c) is a reiteration of "day-labour" in (12b), and that both of these, as well as items such as "bear" in (12d) and "stand and wait" in (12e) are in their turn part of the associative chain of "serve ... serve ... speed ... post ... serve"; it is even more difficult to identify the referential force of items such as "talent", "death", "lodged", "account", "chide" and "his own gifts" that combine with this chain.

The difficulty, of course, lies in the fact that the reader must be able to interpret the rich, biblical allusiveness of (12) – specifically the parable of the talents recorded in Matthew 25: 14-30, but also the allusions to Matthew 11: 30 in (12d) and to the older translation of Psalm 27: 14 in the last words of (12e) – in order to make sense of such associations. Even though there can be no doubt that the biblical references in the poem make up associative networks that give greater coherence to the poem as a whole, Halliday and Hasan's concept of cohesion cannot quite capture this, for these are labelled **exophoric reference** which does not, in their terms, bind together the elements of a text (1976: 18, 37; cf. also 308). Moreover, if cohesion is a relation only between sentences, and not within, then it cannot capture either the increasingly intense syntactic expectation of the climactic question before the main clause in (12b), as, in clause upon clause, the main clause is postponed, or the collocational richness of Milton's poem, especially evident in sentences (12b) ("light ... dark") and (12e) ("speed ... post ...stand ... wait").

After taking a look at how factual lingual texts and the

resources – such as the various types of cohesion – we employ, as lingual subjects, to produce such texts, we return below to some further limitations of the concept of cohesion.

Texts and the idea of lingual economy: a first look

Two general remarks apply to all the types of cohesion discussed above: (a) the employment of the cohesive resources of a language is guided by the regulative lingual principles of lingual economy (cf. Allerton, 1979: 267; also Halliday, 1978: 60 and De Beaugrande & Dressler, 1981: 10f., 60, 64f., 66, 90, 206), i.e. the maxims of being as concise and efficient as possible; (b) a distinction must be made between cohesion as (normative) system of lingual resources that are available to producers of text, and cohesion as (factual) process; between the systematic **potential** or resources of language in ellipsis, reference, substitution and so on, and the **factual, persistent** continuity that these give to a text as its meanings unfold.

The idea of lingual economy will be revisited below (chapter 6) but the conceptual basis of the notion still needs to be clarified. Just as we can form no theoretical concept of a lingual unity within a multiplicity (lingual system and the variety of lingual facts that are regulated by such systems) without seeing the connection between the lingual dimension of reality and the numerical, so we can form no idea of lingual economy without asking what reference makes that possible. The idea of a lingual economy is of course tied to the lingual aspect of experience anticipating or referring forward to the economic dimension of reality (for a graphic representation, see again figure 3.1 in the previous chapter). It provides us with a *regulative* lingual principle because it is related to the linguistic idea that we derive from anticipations of the lingual on those spheres following it, and not a *constitutive* principle, that derives from a reference to an earlier analogy. The idea of lingual economy, we must also note, is no mere metaphor, since the economy being referred to is an economy actually achieved, not just figuratively. The kind of "saving" or frugality with words and syntax that is achieved by using ellipsis, substitution, lexical cohesion, and anaphoric reference is very real, and can be illustrated with reference to real-life lingual facts, as we have seen in our analysis above. Of course, the meaning of the economic dimension of our world is much richer than this, and we shall explore further below the conceptual advantages that this brings also to other references or analogies of the economic in the lingual sphere.

What also needs to be noted is that the distinction that Halliday and Hasan (1976: 18f. and De Beaugrande & Dressler, 1981: 35) make in this connection between the **virtual** system of language and the **actualisation** thereof in text is a distinction that captures once more, though now from a sociolinguistic angle, the differences between lingual norm and lingual fact. It does so in a way that is parallel to the dichotomies of *langue* and *parole*, and **competence** and **performance**, that, as we saw, are employed by formal linguistics (cf. too Halliday, 1978: 133; Halliday & Hasan, 1976: 5, 299).

Some limitations of cohesion as concept

It is precisely the distinction between lingual norm (system) and lingual fact (process) that should remind us that the way we make texts hang together as wholes depends on much more than the employment of the cohesive ties discussed above. Texts have an orderliness that is evidence of their subjection to rules, norms or conventions, and this subjection to a fundamental order of organization is what binds factual texts together.

Where, in terms of the **general** concept of cohesion, a text is an indeterminate, seamless unit without beginning or ending, we all have knowledge of the **typical** conventions that we employ to begin and end specific instances of text, thereby producing texts as individual wholes. For example, the typical "machinery" for speaker selection and the transition of turns between speakers (cf. chapter 6, below) functions as a "fundamental generating feature of conversation" (Schegloff & Sacks, 1973: 294) and seems to be part of the lingual knowledge of normal speakers.

And in order to close conversations, we need to negotiate a well-coordinated, joint ending, as Weideman and Verster (1988) have shown (cf. too Schegloff & Sacks, 1973).

There are numerous other examples of **typical** binding features of texts with which users of the English language are familiar. There are typically different markers of beginning and ending (cf. Allerton, 1979: 282f.) that we all know: in letter writing we begin with our address and end by signing our names, and there is further bracketing of the text between the salutation and the subscription, and even finer distinctions of sub-texts are made by using the devices of paragraphing. Similarly, small advertisements such as

(15) VW BEETLE 1500. 1969. Good mechanic. cond.
In daily use. New tyres. R650 incl GST onco.
Ph A/H 965305.

all seem to begin by stating the make of the car and end with a telephone number. This marking of beginning and ending applies not only to written texts, of course, but also to language that is spoken: Coulthard (1985: 4f.), for example, was one of the earlier analysts to identify the typical structure of a buying transaction, that has a clearly marked beginning and conclusion.

In the Miltonic sonnet that was used above as sample text (12), there is further evidence of such bracketing. The **general** concept of cohesion is not designed to account for the cohesive effects of the rhyme scheme (cf. Halliday & Hasan, 1976: 10), yet it is clear that its use contributes to making this text continuous, i.e. hang together as a whole. Apart from the conventional expectation that the reader might have of the beginning (*abba*) and ending of the rhyme scheme in this kind of sonnet, Milton reinforces our notion of reading/hearing a "bracketed" text by repeating in the arrangement of the *content* of the last four lines the *abba* rhyme *pattern* of the first four: cf. 'state' which indicates lack of movement – a^1; "speed", indicating movement – b^1; "post" signalling movement – b^1, and "stand and wait", again expressing lack of movement – a^1. That the poet also omits the usual mark of punctuation ('.' or ',') between the octave and the sestet in the Petrarchan rhyme scheme, preferring rather to use enjambment between lines 8 and 9, is a further indication of the tight binding together of the poem, and this is indeed what makes it possible to speak of a specific Miltonic (as opposed to Shakespearean or Petrarchan) sonnet form.

Furthermore, the biblical allusion in (12) is not limited to specific biblical texts, such as the parable of the talents in Matthew 25: 14-30, but seems to refer broadly to the basic biblical contours of creation, sin and redemption, since we have 'light' in the first line – almost invariably associated in Milton's work with the *creation* (cf. his *Samson Agonistes* and also Genesis 1: 3) – then there is the poet's sinful *rebellion* (culminating in the foolish question), and, finally, the offer of ultimate *redemption* in the sense of the book of Revelations in the final line: it is a vigilant waiting upon the Lord, keeping an active lookout for Christ's return (cf. Rev. 22: 20) and humankind's final redemption. The employment of these biblical allusions as the **discursive thread** of the poem, echoing the contours of the *first* book of the Bible, that recounts man's creation and rebellion, and the *last*, that prophesies a final redemption, gives still greater **coherence** and unity to the text of (12).

It does not need much further argument (cf. also Carrell, 1982), therefore, to illustrate that the general concept of cohesion does not capture all these typical, sometimes very specific, features of coherence, bracketing, and so forth. It is to make up for this deficiency that the concepts of coherence, register, genre, situation type and the like are introduced, and it is to a discussion of these that attention is finally given.

Possible solutions

Even a less delicate analysis of cohesion in (12) than that proposed by Halliday and Hasan will reveal that this sample text has a remarkable density of cohesive ties (ranging from 1 to 8 ties for every sentence), giving it a very close **texture** (Halliday & Hasan,

1976: 296, 332).[5] There is still greater density if we take cohesion as a systematic resource operating across clause boundaries in the same sentence. Defining ties as occurrences of pairs of cohesively related items, the expectation on the part of Halliday and Hasan (1976: 4, 332) is that in quantifying the different types of tie in a given text, differences in genre will become clear (cf. Visser & Weideman, 1986). The number of ties and types of ties in any given text are not the only basis for identifying and describing genre, however, since this may also be determined by other choices within the systemically available resources, such as the rhetorical modes or functional choices of language use conventionally associated with a genre. In academic discourse, for example, Carstens (2009) has pointed out that **description, discussion, comparison and contrast, persuasion, recount and explanation** all play a role in writing in the humanities.

Cohesion therefore offers a partial descriptive basis for the interpretation of a text, not interpretation *per se* (cf. Hendricks, 1973: 28f., 42). In other words, by describing the *individual* cohesive relations of *specific* texts, the linguistic analysis of text can uncover **recurrent** cohesive relations within a class of texts (a genre) (cf. too Coulthard, 1985: 40f.), which can then on the next level of analysis be generalized in terms of genre theory. So the analysis of cohesion in (12) and (15), for example, could reveal a possible preference in poetic texts for reference, conjunction and lexical cohesion, while at the same time it would show a preference for extra-ordinarily elliptical forms in the genre of the small advertisement (for findings on other genres, cf. Visser & Weideman, 1986; Smith & Crawley, 1983). But the failure of other methods of quantification (cf. De Beaugrande & Dressler, 1981: 183) should make us cautious to expect too much. Also, one must remember that our expectations of what makes (12) different from (15) may in the first instance derive not so much from the identification and quantification of cohesive ties, as from the informal labels "poetic language" and "small advertisement" that are intuitively assigned to these *before* any theoretical analysis takes place.

---

5. The Afrikaans and Dutch words for writing poetry, "dig" en "dichten" (lit.: "making dense") exactly capture this quality.

A more reasonable line to pursue in order to discover the typically **coherent** (as opposed to generally cohesive) features of different classes of text would perhaps be to invoke the notion of **register** (cf. Halliday, 1978: 150; Halliday & Hasan, 1976: 26ff.) to define such classes. Cohesion is therefore supplemented by a concept of register, which can be defined as the configuration of semantic resources that is **typically** associated with a situation type, i.e. the meaning potential of a **typical** social context (Halliday, 1978: 111; also 123, 183; cf. too Hymes's associated concept of a verbal or communicative repertoire [1971: 277, 290]). Whereas the cohesive potential of English has a catalytic, enabling function in the meaning potential of a language, the concept of register, in its turn, is "the necessary mediating concept between a text and its sociosemiotic environment" (Halliday, 1978: 145); it is the *janus*-concept that links text to a typical social context or situation type.[6]

Through the use of the **general** meaning potential of language, of which the textual function, including the cohesive resources of language, is a part, and by the employment of the **typical** resources of register and our knowledge of different types of discourse functioning within typical social contexts, we are able to create texts as individual wholes possessing a particular kind of identity or individuality structure. The semantic system of language is the interface between language and the social world, between language conceived as general system and language as typical institution (Halliday & Hasan, 1976: 305; Halliday, 1978: 183). Together, these concepts – cohesion, coherence, genre, register and typical social contexts in which specific types of discourse operate – constitute an answer to the question of how lingual subjects produce texts that hang together; as theoretical concepts and ideas, they allow us to clarify our pre-theoretical perceptions and intuitions that differentiate between texts that are legal, poetic, instructional, scientific, religious, etc., in nature.

---

6. Cf. too Hymes's (1971: 290) "domains of communicative behaviour".

In short, such ideas present linguistic theory with a means of making it theoretically respectable to talk, for example, of the **typically** juridical, aesthetic, technical, analytical or confessional identity of texts, while at the same time we need never lose sight of the **general** features of textual continuity. Both of the subsequent chapters consider, though from slightly different perspectives, ideas related to the connectedness of (especially spoken) texts.

5 The analysis of discourse in English

Text linguistics, conversation analysis and discourse analysis

There are a number of competing and complementary approaches to the analysis of the structure and organization of discourse in English. All of these attempt, in formal or non-formal (functional) terms, to describe the principles that condition and determine factual texts produced by lingual subjects engaged in some social encounter (**text linguistics**), or to clarify, like **conversation analysis**, which we shall consider in the next chapter, the way that participants at talk arrange their collaborative effort sequentially, from one turn to the next, by taking certain (normative) rules as points of orientation for such organization.

In this chapter, we wish to consider another way of analyzing the organization and structure of lingual interaction in English, namely discourse analysis. What it has in common with the others mentioned above is that it is an attempt to discover structure and organization in lingual objects and events that lie beyond the sentence. As we shall see, the way that it achieves this differs on several counts from the methods employed in conversation analysis, the analytical method that will be considered in the next chapter. As Levinson (1983: 286) points out, discourse analysis essentially strives to extend the techniques that have been employed in formal linguistic analyses to make them apply supra-sententially. In this sense it is characterized by an initial, hypothetical definition of different units of discourse, that are subsequently arranged in a hierarchical ("consists of") relation. For example, where in formal linguistics there is a hierarchy of formal units starting, usually, with the phoneme, morpheme and word, that builds up hierarchically to the formation of phrase, clause and sentence, several approaches in discourse analysis hypothesize that there is, in any type of discourse, different higher levels of organization that "consist of" lower ones. So, Coulthard (1985: 123ff.) discusses the organization of discourse in terms of the levels of

> transaction
> exchange
> move
> act

where transaction, the highest unit, is said to consist of two or more exchanges, exchanges consist of two or more moves, and moves in turn consist of a specifiable set or combination of acts. This is not at all the way that conversation analysis proposes to set about its analytical task, for it claims that it starts without any preconceived notion of structure, finding this only after devoting meticulous attention to recurrent patterns occurring over a number of texts. What is discovered in such an analysis that "emerge(s) from observation of the conduct of the participants" (Heritage & Atkinson, 1984: 1; cf. also Sacks, 1984) is an underlying orderliness which co-participants at talk regularly and methodically subject themselves to, and, importantly, to which they know they orient themselves in the ongoing process of talk.

There are two observations to be made in this regard:

(a) First, no theory, or, for that matter, theoretical analysis can start "from scratch", without preconceptions. This is also true of conversation analysis, however much it is claimed to arise from the "naturally occurring" data itself. In one of the earliest studies in conversation analysis, for example, Sacks, Schegloff & Jefferson (1974: 697f., note 5) refer to the idea of taking turns, and, hence, to the sequentiality of talk, right at the very outset of their study, noting that it goes back to ideas already discussed 40 years before. This means, secondly, that, having once "discovered" this sequential organization in talk, subsequent analyses confirm or reconfirm their existence. Hence Heritage & Atkinson (1984: 5) acknowledge that in conversation analysis

it is sequences and turns within sequences ...
that have become the primary units of analysis.

However "natural" or "dirty" the material is in which such units are discovered, in other words, the analysis remains firmly within the tradition of abstraction which is part and parcel of theoretical analysis, to operate in terms of distinct units of analysis (cf. also Weideman, 1985b), even to the extent of acknowledging that turns constitute sequences, or, put in discourse analytical terms, sequences consist of turns (Heritage & Atkinson, 1984: 6). What is more, conversation analysts today acknowledge that transcriptions of "naturally occurring conversation" are "necessarily selective" in that the transcription system employed is "particularly concerned with capturing the sequential features of talk" (Heritage & Atkinson, 1984: 12). The apparent similarity of discourse and conversation analytical distinctions with regard to each operating in terms of units of analysis has led to a number of attempts to achieve a fusion of the two (cf. e.g. Edmondson, 1981). What is important to observe, from our point of view, is the impossibility to conceptualize lingual phenomena without reference to the analogies of other dimensions within the lingual. In this case, we have the concept of a (potential) multiplicity of factual lingual units that are subject to or regulated by a system of lingual norms. What the units are called may vary; the fact is, we cannot conceptualize and analyze discourse if we do not identify such units in terms of which we may do so.

(b) The major difference between conversation analysis and discourse analysis on this score, however, is that the discovered units exhibit a sequential organization which is recognized as such also by those who produce them. Conversation analysis, Sacks (1984: 21) says, "seeks to describe methods persons use in doing social life." This is not necessarily the case in a discourse analytical perspective, where the different units of discourse, on whatever level (act, move, exchange, etc.) are linked from a perspective that takes a greater hypothetical distance from the material than that of the participants engaged in producing them.

Discourse analysis also has much in common with the first mode of analysis referred to above, viz. text linguistics. Where part of text linguistics, specifically studies in the area of cohesion (cf. Halliday & Hasan, 1976), is concerned with formal links between the various sentences/utterances in a spoken or written text, much attention is also given, as we have noted, to a non-formal or functional explanation of discourse. In such explanations of the organization of discourse a critical feature appears to be the coherence of a stretch of text, i.e. the non-arbitrary connectedness or continuity that enables the participants in a lingual encounter to interpret such a text as a whole, even where verbally explicit or formal connections are absent. If one looks at the contents of discourse analysis textbooks (cf., e.g., Brown & Yule, 1983), one is immediately struck by the prominence which the idea of coherence is accorded. We shall therefore be devoting attention below to the coherence of, as well as to the functional explanations for, lingual events and objects.

Frames, scripts, scenarios and schemata

A set of near synonymous concepts that are used in the field of discourse analysis to describe the coherence of a given stretch of text is that of **frame, script, scenario and schema**. All of these intend to describe, in marginally different ways, how we perceive, produce or process (i.e. understand) a given text as one unit of discourse.

A **frame** can be defined as "a fixed representation of knowledge about the world" (Brown & Yule, 1983: 239) that enables the analyst to describe this coherence. As a concept, it is linked with work in memory research, i.e. it states that when we encounter a new text, we manage to understand it in terms of a framework that represents a data structure in our memory which is composed of previously encountered, **stereotyped** situations. For example, when we encounter a text such as

(1)   IMPORTANT
        Please read this first
        Guarantee certificate
        Date of purchase ....
        Invoice no. ....
        Dealer's name ....
        Dealer's address ....

we know, from previous experience and from the stereotypical way in which this has been presented to us, that what we have here is part of a manufacturer's guarantee, probably for some kind of (household) appliance or piece of machinery. This is evident not only from the fact that this is explicitly stated ("Guarantee certificate"), but also from the other information, such as date of purchase, dealer's name, etc., that is given. Similarly, when we read a text such as

(2)   AL-KO SHREDDER Compost Star 1100
        A.S.T. System
        Gebrauchsanweisung
        Operating Instructions
        Mode d'emploi
        Instruzioni d'uso
        Handleiding

we would know, from remembered data structures that we have encountered before, that what we can expect on the first page is something like

(2a) General points on shredding and composting

or something similar. In other words, even if the title had not been given also in English, but only in German, French, Italian and Dutch, the format of the booklet, the caption ("AL-KO SHREDDER ...") and perhaps even the (to this reader uninterpretable) "A.S.T. system" would, from more or less similar past experiences of such literature, have enabled us to make sense of (2) as the lead-in or title page of an instruction booklet.

The notion of our understanding a text in the light of expectations that we have is also covered in the idea of **script.** Unlike a frame, which captures a more or less static and stable state of affairs, the idea of a script attempts to accommodate an expected (sequence) of events (Brown & Yule, 1983: 243). So, one may expect to hear, in the slot marked "x" in (3)

(3) B: I grew up around horses. So ..
    K: Is that where you learned x?

(adapted from Craig & Tracy, 1983: 315) something like "to ride" (as in the actual conversation from which this was taken), but, equally plausible in conceptual terms, also perhaps "to groom horses", "to hunt", "to jump", and so forth. Of course, the strong expectations that we have may lead us to understandings that are quite wrong, and which, in real language use, have to be overcome, often in a negotiation of meaning between participants at talk. Here is an example, once again from a transcribed conversation, in which the one participant's expectations of why he is being given a particular piece of information leads him to complete the turn (marked *) of the other participant with a statement that turns out to be erroneous:

(4) A: But the Faculty of Arts has eh a sort of supreme Soviet
    B: Mhm
    A: which is called the Board of the faculty
    B: Yes
    A: and
*   B: you're on that
    A: No..o, no, no, Dave is
    B: Dave is on that, ah
            (adapted from Svartvik & Quirk, 1980: 81).

So strong are our ("scripted") expectations that researchers have found that when someone is presented with a text in which actions are purposely scrambled so as not to occur in an expectable sequence, such a person will, upon recalling the text, restore it to a more predictable order (Brown & Yule, 1983: 245). In other words, the notion of script has what is known in the literature as "psychological reality".

The third of these concepts, **scenario**, concerns background knowledge of settings and environments that allow the receiver of a text to interpret it (Brown & Yule, 1983: 245). Again, the notion has to do with the perceptual speed or ease with which we interpret texts given their occurrence against the backdrop of a given scenario. In one of the examples cited by Brown & Yule (1983: 246), researchers claim that it takes longer for readers to process the target sentence in (5a) than in (5b):

(5a)   Title: Telling a lie
         Fred was being questioned.
         He couldn't tell the truth.

         Target: The lawyer was trying to prove his innocence.

(5b)   Title: In court
         Fred was being questioned.
         He had been accused of murder.

         Target: The lawyer was trying to prove his innocence.

The reason given for the same target sentence being interpreted with greater ease and speed in the second case is that here a specific scenario ("In court") has been activated, while in the first text (5a) there is a much vaguer, general scenario.

It is this specificity that distinguishes the term "scenario" from **schemata**, which are "more general types of knowledge representations" (Brown & Yule, 1983: 247). Like the other concepts dealt with here, schemata have to do with the background knowledge that enables us to predict or expect certain things while we are interpreting a given text (Brown & Yule,1983: 248). An example cited by Brown & Yule (1983: 248) is again pertinent. In one experiment, text (6) below was given to two groups of students, the one consisting of a number of female students studying music, and the other of male students from a weight-lifting class:

(6) Every Saturday night, four good friends get together. When Jerry, Mike and Pat arrived, Karen was sitting in her living room writing some notes. She quickly gathered the cards and stood up to greet her friends at the door. They followed her into the living room but as usual they couldn't agree on exactly what to play. Jerry eventually took a stand and set things up. Finally, they began to play. Karen's recorder filled the room with soft and pleasant music. Early in the evening, Mike noticed Pat's hand and the many diamonds ...

Predictably, the music students interpreted the text as one describing a musical evening, there having been sufficient clues in the text to activate a discursive schema to back up such an interpretation. The men students, on the other hand, thought that the story was about four friends playing cards together, again basing their interpretation on certain clues in the text. What this demonstrates, in other words, is that our background knowledge and interests predispose us to entertain certain interpretations of a text, and to ignore others.

All of these concepts, however, in some way approximate what we have been calling the **normative expectations** that guide and accompany our understanding of texts produced within a social relationship that has its own, unique **type of discourse**. More than anything else, it is our (socio-lingual) knowledge of different types of discourse that will enable us to distinguish (7) from (8) as belonging respectively to an interviewing session and a classroom, or both of these from (4) above, which apparently is a stretch of conversation:

(7) A: Now obviously the viruses all differ. We have different

viruses through the years. How do you know which virus is the one to vaccinate against?

B: Well, three viruses are important ones this year and they are the ones that have been put into this vaccine. The Department of Health and Population Development have categorically stated that the Chilean, Philippean and Russian. strains must be used and these are the three strains that are in this vaccine.

A: How is this decision made?

B: It's made on an international basis. Yearly it's upgraded and there are people that watch for the outbreaks of influenza round the world and anticipate those particular strains coming to a particular country.

A: So they would have been particularly serious in Europe and North America for example this last winter.

B: Correct.

(Transcription made available by I. Langenhoven)

(8) A: Right. Now if you had a holiday like that, where would you go? What would you do?
(Several bids)
A: If you could go anywhere? (nominates B)
B: I'd go camping.
A: Right. Somebody would go camping.
(Greyling, 1987: 221)

This same knowledge of discourse type would likewise enable us to recognize (9) as belonging to the same type of discourse as (8), even though it appears, on closer scrutiny, to deviate somewhat from the conventional expectation we have of classroom talk:

(9) A: Sir, you still have some of our blocks.
B: Your blocks. Do I still have some of your blocks?
A: Yeah.
B: How many do I have to give you?
A: Two white ones and a red.
B: (non-verbal: gives them the blocks) Two white ones

and a red. That's it.

(Greyling, 1987: 249f.)

In order to arrive at a more precise characterization of different types of discourse, it is necessary to look more closely at the different functions of various possible acts, combinations of these in moves, and to possible exchange types in each, since it is to these that much of our experience of such typical differences can be attributed. This will be considered in the next section.

Discourse function

One of the most commonly acknowledged notions in various discussions of discourse analysis is that our lingual actions can only be explained by relating them to the **function**(s) that they fulfil in communication. Indeed, Sinclair & Coulthard's (1975) definition of the various discourse acts appeals in the first instance to the function that such acts have in relation to others. So, for example, the acts Elicitation and Directive are distinguishable in discourse as acts that respectively function to request a linguistic (i.e. verbal) response or to request a non-linguistic (i.e. non-verbal) response (Burton, 1980: 157). In their turn, two of the responding acts, Reply and React, function respectively to provide a verbal response to a preceding Elicitation, and to give a non-verbal response to a Directive (Burton, 1980: 158). We take a look first at a set of Reacts that constitute responses, in a stretch of classroom talk, to a series of Directives used in conjunction with Informatives, another kind of act:

(10) (Pupils walk into classroom; they go to their groups;
     equipment for experiment ready)
   T: Please put your cases on the floor. You've got lots of
      space. (d, i)
   Ps: (NV: they do as they are told) (rea)
   T: Try and face this way. It will be easier to see
      what's going on. (d, i)
   Ps: (NV: pupils do as they are told) (rea)

T: I think it will be easier, Street, if you go over there -
   or Gleason, you go over there - it will be easier. (i, d, d, i)

(Greyling, 1987: 257)

In the same way (11) contains instances of the act of Elicitation followed by a Reply:

(11) T: And how is the current going to pass through
       the copper chloride solution? (el)
    P: The ions. (rep)
    T: Ions. (e)
       What about the ions? (el)
    P: Movement of charge. (rep)
    T: Movement of charge (e)

(Greyling, 1987: 257f.)

In fact, in (11) we see not only a pattern of exchange between T (teacher) and P (pupil) that consists of Elicitations followed by Replies, but also note a third act, that of Evaluate, that the teacher uses, in this case, to signal agreement with the Reply of the pupil. The pattern of acts that emerges from this stretch of classroom talk is, in other words,

Elicitation - Reply - Evaluate - Elicitation - Reply - Evaluate

where the Elicitation and Evaluate are acts on the part of the teacher, and Reply is a pupil act. These acts make up, on the next level of analysis, a **move structure** in an elicitative exchange that has the familiar

Initiation - Response - Feedback

or IRF pattern that Sinclair & Coulthard (1975) found to be the most frequently occurring one in classroom discourse. In (12) below, we see an optional extension of this move sequencing within a similar kind of exchange to form the following pattern:

Initiation - Bid - Nomination - Response - Feedback

(12) T: Give me an example in a sentence. (el; Initiation)
    P: That lady is old. (rep; Response)
    T: That lady is old. Good. (e, acc; Feedback)
       What else? (el; Initiation)
    Ps: (NV: bids) (Bid)
    T: (NV: nominates pupil) Yes (n; Nomination)
    P: Late. (rep; Response)
    T: Late. No. (e, acc; Feedback)
                   (Greyling, 1987: 305f.)

Of course, depending on the kind of class (and the disciplinary style of the teacher), not all classroom talk is as tidily arranged as this: in (13), for example, it takes a while for the teacher to resume control of the talk, i.e. in assigning turns at talk or to determine who speaks next (and even what would count as an allowable contribution in such a next turn):

(13) T: Can you tell me specifically what charges .. what ions are in fact going to move in this solution? (Initiation)
   Ps: (Inaudible. Answers are shouted out) (Chaos of responses)
    T: Don't shout it out! (cue)
   Ps: (Immediate silence; bidding is done simultaneously) (Bid)
    T: (NV: nominates pupil by pointing at him) Yes. (Nomination)
    P: Sir, uh, the copper, the positive copper ion and the negative chloride ion (Response)
    T: The negative chloride ion and the positive chloride ion ... (Feedback)
                 (Greyling, 1987: 258f.)

Nonetheless, an extended IRF move pattern, that now includes (teacher) Initiation - (pupil) Bid - (teacher) Nomination - (pupil) Response - (teacher) Feedback is still very much in evidence in this teacher-pupil exchange. Apart from these elicitative types of exchanges, there is in classroom talk also one other exchange type which is of crucial importance, since this one demarcates the boundaries of exchanges, signalling the terminals of a series of exchanges in a transaction. No doubt we are familiar with the following examples taken, again, from real samples of classroom talk (Weideman, 1985c: 3f.):

(14) a. Now, what I want you to do is just remember this ...
b. Now, if we look on the board here ...
c. Right, can we quickly try this one ...
d. Right, uh ... today, let us take a look at another kind of exercise ...

These kinds of moves, a Frame followed (usually) by a Focussing move, belong to the class of Boundary exchanges in the terminology of discourse analysis.

How well does the system of discourse analysis designed by Coulthard, Sinclair and other co-workers on the Birmingham project describe classroom talk? There is no doubt that it can handle fairly well any conventional teacher-pupil lingual interaction in the classroom, perhaps with some modification and refinement as has been suggested in later work. In what follows, we shall take a look at some more unconventional patterns in classroom talk, specifically where these are caused by new developments in teaching techniques and methods, and also look at one attempt at applying this system of analysis to a type of discourse other than classroom talk.

Unconventional patterns in discourse

As a first example of unconventional classroom talk we take (15):

(15) T: ... You build the thing on this side ... Let's hear what it sounds like.
P: Take a red block and a white block and place them on the table next to each other ...

What is unusual here, when compared to conventional class-room talk, is of course that one has a (Teacher) Directive and Elicitation followed not by a React or Reply, but by a Directive. Moreover, this is a pupil Directive. There is no doubt that this Directive is a response, but the sequential placement is unexpected, and its functioning as a response is not covered by the definition given by Sinclair and Coulthard (1975: 41), who explicitly state that its function is to request a non-linguistic response, and not, in other words, to be a linguistic response. The same problem occurs in (16):

> (16) T: Here's a problem. I think you'll have to start again.
> P1: Take a red one and a white one. Put them down flat on the table ... (explanation continues) ... Have you got it?
> P2: Yes.
> P1: Then you take the red one and put it in exactly the same position on the other side.
> P2: Yes.

After the (expected) Initiation move by the teacher, one finds again a series of pupil Directives, before, upon an unexpected pupil Check ("Have you got it?") another pupil contributes a response. In the last two moves in (16), pupil l's Directive ("Then you take the red one ...") is followed not only by an untranscribed React, but also by a verbal response. Again, this is not provided for in Sinclair and Coulthard's description, where Directives are not followed by verbal responses.

Another problem for this model for the analysis of discourse is evident in the obviously different functions that conventional teacher questions have when one compares them with other, "real" questions. As is well known, a question from a teacher is not in the first instance designed to elicit information that the teacher does not know, but rather to determine whether a pupil or pupils know the answer. A genuine information-seeking question, however, such as "How many do I have to give you?" in (9), repeated here as (17), does not have this characteristic.

(17) P: Sir, you still have some of our blocks.
      T: Your blocks. Do I still have some of your blocks?
      P: Yeah.
      T: How many do I have to give you?
      P: Two white ones and a red.
      T: (non-verbal: gives them the blocks) Two white ones
      and a red. That's it.

(Greyling, 1987: 249f.)

The teacher is, however, still in control of what is happening, as is evident from the last contribution above ("That's it"), as well as in those cases where pupils take the opportunity of putting a question to the teacher, as in (18) below:

(18) P: What is the idea of Public Support?
      T: Right. Here is a question if you want to listen
         to it. What is the idea of Public Support? The
         only way that you can stop wasting Ergs, right?
         Because every time ... (explanation continues) ...

(Weideman, 1985c: 5)

However, to the untrained observer, it would be difficult if not impossible to determine who is the teacher in texts such as (19), (20) and (21) below (Weideman, 1985c: 6):

(19) A: What are those cards called?
      B: These are research and development cards.

(20) A: How do you move?
      B: You move either ... right .. there are two ways,
         two ways of moving. One is with the dice.

(21) C: OK. You need .. on the system chart all those ...
         all the numbers one to three are all advantages.
         Now the research and development cards - you
         must try to change all of these here. Uh ..
         you must try (continues explanation) ...

In order to make sense of these texts as examples of classroom talk, one needs to know the precise context as well as the allocation of roles between the participants. In both (19) and (20), participant A, though apparently the initiator of the exchange, is the pupil. The questions asked in these exchanges are information-seeking questions on the part of pupils, who are about to attempt to play a cooperative board game as part of a language teaching lesson, and have been allowed by the teacher to ask two questions before they begin. This is, of course, not a strictly conventional situation, which explains some of the difficulties in interpreting (19) and (20). It is significant to note, however, that if one places each of these into their broader lingual context, the teacher's control of the discourse is still evident, although now not on a local, turn-by-turn basis. The point, therefore, is that classroom talk does not always conform to our expectation of teacher-initiated Initiation-Response-Feedback (IRF) type exchanges. This is clear also in (21), where someone not familiar with the context could easily misinterpret C's explanation as being the teacher's. It is, however, that of a pupil trying to explain the rules and objectives of the same cooperative board game to other pupils.

An unconventional pattern of classroom discourse is to be found not only in language teaching classrooms, from which most of these examples have been taken, but also in others. Who, for example, is the teacher in (22)? The excerpt is from a transcription made by Richmond (1982: 201):

(22) T: What's that inside there? What's it called?
      K: Copper sulphate.
      S: Right then now have you lit the Bunsen burner?
          No you haven't.
      T: We need splints, oh yeah splints and we
          haven't even lit it yet.
      B: What do you want splints for?
      T: To light it. Yeah, I can't put a lighter down on
          the apparatus can I?
      B: Say a cigarette then.

C: Er ...
T: And what are those called? I've forgotten ...
K: Now keep it settling for a few minutes over a slow flame.

T is very likely to be the first candidate we would consider for the role of teacher. She starts with a question that closely resembles "typical" teacher elicitations. However, later on T also answers a question from B, which seems an unlikely action on the part of a teacher. Then there is S's teacher-like framing move to consider: "Right then now have you lit ..." Since the teacher is evidently not C, who only makes a minimal contribution, S becomes an even more likely candidate. But what about K? K initiates what looks like the beginning of a Teacher Direct-exchange (Sinclair & Coulthard, 1975: 50f.): "Now keep it settling ..." The problem that we have when we take K to be the teacher, however, is that she has also in her first contribution responded in a way that is more normal for pupils than for teachers. It would come as a surprise to most who are unfamiliar with talk in classrooms where collaborative effort in carrying out a task is required, to learn that the teacher is neither K nor S, but B. This is Mr Bellini, the natural science teacher, who is monitoring the progress of an experiment being done by a group of pupils (Trina, Kim, Sally and Carole).

There is no doubt that the model of discourse analysis we are discussing would have to be adapted and modified, perhaps even substantially, before it could cope with the analysis of such texts. Particularly its ability to cope with the analysis of classroom talk where pupils contribute more than the conventional single turn out of every three would have to be examined, as well as what would constitute allowable sequences or combinations of acts. One attempt at its modification that appears to have been done more or less successfully is that of Burton (1980), who tried to apply the analysis to drama dialogue. Here is one section of the analysis (Burton, 1980: 160):

CHALLENGING MOVE	OPENING MOVE	SUPPORTING MOVE
	B: Kaw Frame in	
G: He what? e	What about this? S Listen to this! S A man of 87 wanted to cross the road i But there was a lot of traffic see ... So he crawled under a lorry	
	B: He crawled under a lorry rep A stationary lorry	G: No? ack
	B: The lorry started and ran over him	G: Go on! ack B: That's what it says here com G: Get away! ack

What is immediately evident is that sequentially occurring contributions by different participants are not necessarily fitted into different columns (for moves). Thus G's act of acknowledgement, analyzed as a Supporting move, is itself supported by another from B, and followed by another from G, and so on. The major modification that has been made, therefore, seems to be the division of moves into Opening, Supporting and Challenging moves (Burton, 1980: 142). This is in keeping not only with our intuitions on how discourse progresses, but also echoes the interactional moves identified by Edmondson (1981: 86ff.) as Proffer, Satisfy and Counter (or Contra).

Edmondson (1981: 169) has also added a refinement to the overall organization of discourse, which has the following structure (cf. that of Coulthard, above):

Encounter
Phase

Exchange
Move
Act

Encounters, at the highest level, are therefore made up of one or more Phases, Phases consist of Exchanges, Exchanges of Moves, and Moves of one or various Acts. The underlying idea is much the same as that of Sinclair and Coulthard (1975), though it is now generalized for all kinds of discourse (cf. the replacement of the rank of "Lesson" with the more neutral "Encounter"). Such a generally applicable structure for discourse is what analyses such as those discussed here most often attempt. Such models provide one with an initial way of getting to grips with the workings of discourse in various environments. What they need to be complemented with if we are to discover what makes various types of discourse unique, however, is the distinction between institutional, associational and communal settings for talk, as well as an idea of the nature of the kind of talk produced within a given sphere of discourse.

The type of distinctions set out in this chapter constitutes the basis and historical beginnings of discourse analysis. Since that time, the study of discourse has grown and developed, to include not only fine-grained analyses such as these attempted by various theorists in this chapter, but also to encompass wider societal issues, such as the study of how political power manifests itself in the lingual interactions of lingual subjects. Critical discourse analysis, as the study of these (often unequal) interactions is called, has alerted us to how inequality and (political) discrimination affects our lingual interactions, and how such inequality is either strengthened by our insensitivity in handling such discourse, or resisted and overcome when we become sensitive to how we construct our social identities in language. Though this whole field lies outside of the scope of an introduction to linguistics such as this, we turn in the next chapter to another way of looking at the distribution of talk across lingual subjects.

6 Conversation analysis and the maintenance of talk

Social anticipations in the lingual aspect

We are able to grasp the linkages between the lingual dimension of reality and the other aspects in terms of two sets of analogies, that either look back towards earlier aspects (retrocipations), or that look forward, as anticipatory moments. The former set yields constitutive linguistic concepts, the latter provides a set of limiting concepts or regulative linguistic ideas. As we have noted in the previous chapters, the analysis of the social analogies in the structure of the lingual aspect are forward-looking, anticipatory moments. By forward-looking, we mean that through these analogies we are able to see how the lingual dimension of reality is opened up or disclosed by referring to an idea or set of ideas beyond the lingual, or at least beyond the constitutive concepts of the lingual aspect of our experience that we have analysed in the various formal approaches to linguistics dealt with in chapter 2.

The social anticipations within the lingual yield a linguistic idea, or actually a whole set of ideas. Our analysis of these anticipatory, disclosing moments allows us, for example, to grasp notions of lingual **spheres of discourse**, each with their own normative requirements, that variously determine the factual lingual **text types** that operate within them. Furthermore, we find here ideas of lingual **informativity** and **acceptability** or appropriateness, which are once more related to the differentiated number of spheres of discourse (cf. too Weideman, 2009: Chapter 14) that operate in our varied social lives. What is informative, acceptable or appropriate in one sphere may not necessarily be so in another: there is a variety, which is a socially differentiated variety, that is at play here. To take an easy example: the syntax and terse vocabulary of a text message sent on a mobile phone, though socially appropriate and acceptable, might not be acceptable as an academic or legal text. In these cases, there are socially variable types of discourse, each with their own set of norms that typify the general notions of acceptability and appropriateness.

The disclosure of the lingual aspect by dimensions following it does not stop at the social sphere. Beyond the social, as is clear from the diagram below, we have economic, aesthetic, juridical, and other dimensions that may be reflected within the structure of the lingual. Each of these yields its own regulative linguistic idea: the ideas of lingual economy (economic anticipation within the lingual), lingual harmony (aesthetic disclosure), lingual ratification, accountability and redress (juridical moments), and so on.

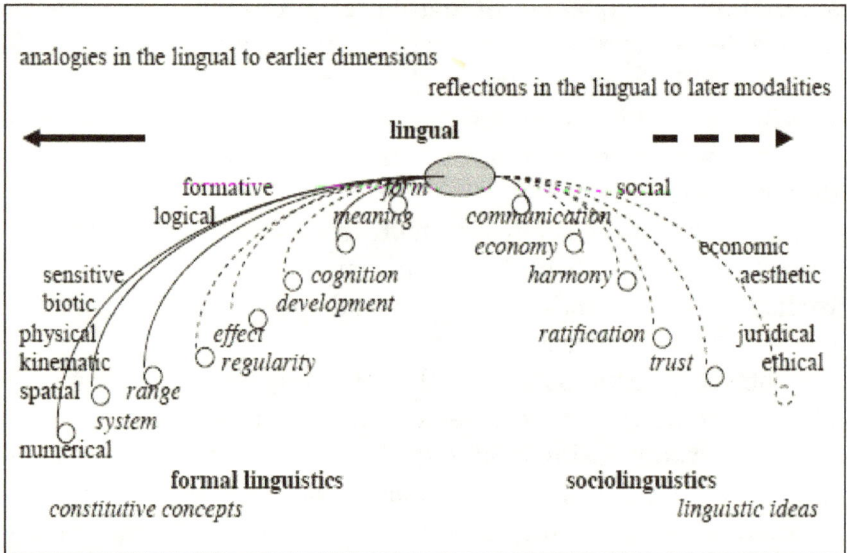

Figure 6.1: Formal linguistic concepts and sociolinguistic ideas

The main purpose of the current chapter is to take a linguistic idea, that of lingual economy, further along the analytical track that has been indicated by the systematic framework briefly described above. As will be shown, the notion of lingual economy cannot be understood without reference to other analogical relations. In fact, all these analogies together deepen the systematic exploration, as well as our understanding, of the others. In a very specific sense, the idea of lingual economy that will be systematically articulated below enhances our understanding of the social disclosure of language in different material lingual spheres, which I have touched upon in the previous chapters, and which is also discussed in detail in Weideman (2009: Chapters 4 and 14). Below, I shall freely use the material and analyses that are discussed in a broader context and detail elsewhere (Weideman, 1988: Chapter 5; 2009: Chapter 15).

The main point to be made here is that the idea of a lingual economy is a regulative idea, in which the lingual aspect of experience anticipates the economic dimension. In addition, it is mediated through the social anticipations or analogies within the lingual aspect.

The idea of lingual economy

There are, naturally, all kinds of intuitive and practical, everyday notions associated with the idea of lingual economy. One may think, for example, of judgments we make of an interlocutor's loquaciousness or taciturnity, or of the more intellectually sophisticated assessments we might make of the economy of expression that is associated with certain forms of verbal art, in particular with poetry and poetic expression, which achieves a remarkable density through its utilization of a number of lingual and other symbolic resources.

Then there is of course the further temptation to conceive of the analogical modal link between the lingual dimension of our experience and the economic dimension of reality in terms of the concrete phenomenon of language and its role in the sphere of economic life, in other words in the world of trade, commerce and financial transactions. In our time, for example, English has gained enormously in importance globally, as has Mandarin. These are no doubt interesting issues. The way that language acts as barrier to commerce and trade, or the way in which economic considerations influence the power that some languages gain on a global scale, while others stand to lose, are complex issues that are studied within the realm of language management or planning, as well as in language politics. These issues are therefore more properly treated in the latter sub-fields of applied linguistics (or in development economics, as Van Langevelde, 1997 and 1999 have done for Friesland and minority regions).

Instead, the analysis below will be limited first to an illustration of how, in the theoretical approach known as ethnomethodology (cf. Sacks, Schegloff & Jefferson, 1974; Goffman, 1981; Sacks, 1984; Schegloff, 1992, 2001; Atkinson & Heritage, 1984; Schegloff & Sacks, 1973), a breakaway school of sociology, we find a theoretically exceptional treatment of the idea of lingual economy. Their analyses enlighten us as regards the wonderfully complicated nature of lingual interaction when our theoretical view ventures beyond the consideration of the expressive kernel of the lingual modality to an analysis of the structuredness of the shared expression or communication that lingual subjects attempt every day. The analysis engages first with a social analogy within the structure of the lingual aspect. If shared expression or communication provides the starting point for this analysis, it situates the lingual facts that are brought into view squarely within the social domain, or what I have been calling the social anticipations of the lingual aspect. That, in turn, immediately places spoken interaction in the theoretical spotlight. In pointing out the differences between Grice's (1975) 'theory-driven' methodology and that of the 'data-driven' approach of the ethnomethodologists, Svennevig (2001) is correct in observing that our

> claims about spoken interaction are based on theoretical primitives (such as *meaning, rationality* and *communication*).

110

The 'primitives' that Svennevig has in mind indeed are foundational linguistic concepts that express the connections between the lingual dimension and, respectively, the logical aspect of experience (in the concepts of factual lingual identity, rationality or meaning) and the social (lingual expression that is shared with others to deepen into communication). However, we shall see that the articulation by ethnomethodologists of the idea of a lingual economy operating in spoken interaction proceeds from just such a 'primitive' or foundational linguistic idea. In this case the 'primitive' is grounded in the anticipation by the lingual of the economic aspect of reality.

In the illustration of lingual economy that will be dealt with below, lingual economy will be conceptualized as a factual scarcity of a lingual resource. This scarce resource is identified in ethnomethodological analysis as a turn at talk. The problem of scarcity is resolved, especially in one form of talk, conversation, with reference to its more or less equal distribution. Such equal distribution is achieved through the orientation that we have, as speakers, to a normative lingual system for sharing or distributing this scarce resource. In this formulation, the idea of lingual economy refers both to the 'capitalist' notion of economy (scarcity) and the 'socialist' idea of achieving (equitable) distribution. The system of turn-taking that will be referred to below thus encapsulates both 'scarcity' and 'distribution'.

In the illustration that follows, I shall also freely use some earlier material and analyses that I have made individually or in collaboration with others (Weideman, 1984, 1985b, 1988; Weideman, Raath & Van der Walt, 1986; Weideman & Verster, 1988).

A system for lingual sharing

The analyses that the school of ethnomethodology made have been particularly useful for us in gaining insight into the normative dimensions of our communicative ability to function as lingual subjects within one specific type of discourse, conversation. These insights have taken us much further than the initial, preliminary analyses of conversation done by Crystal and Davy (1969), where the overall impression is that conversation is 'random', forever edging towards indeterminacy and chaos. Most of the examples cited in this early study are of a lexical and syntactic nature; that is, they use factual lingual units at word and sentence level.

We should note, however, that once we take the study of human lingual competence and action beyond the notion of grammatical competence, other considerations emerge, and other levels of lingual object-formation than for the lexical and syntactic level come into play. Thus it is with the analysis of conversation. The unit of analysis here will be a turn at talk, not a sentence, or even an utterance.

If we take a turn at talk as a lingual unit, we shall soon see that, far from being random, unpredictable and indeterminate, as was initially thought, conversation analysis will show such talk to have a remarkably tight and economical organization. The idea of turn-taking in conversation is therefore central to this analysis. It is of course true that the lingual economy that is effected by means of turn-taking among those sharing in communicative interaction is not limited to conversation. Conversation is only one form of talk: that which is conducted among equals in an associative relationship. In most forms of talk, done within the various material lingual spheres of discourse (Weideman, 2009), some normative system of turn-taking is indeed operative. So for example the allocation of turns at talk in a classroom has been investigated by Greyling (1987; cf. too Coulthard, 1985; Duff, 2002; Storch, 2004; Arthur & Martin, 2006) and others. When we looked at analyses of classroom discourse in the previous chapter, we saw that the inequality in this form of institutional talk is such that in conventional classrooms the teacher normally occupies two-thirds of this scarce resource, in initiating a typical exchange by eliciting information, and ending it by giving feedback to the learner's response. Similarly, in ecclesiastical settings, which make up another institutional context, there may be predetermined and liturgically or ritually specified measures of how turns at talk are distributed. Parliamentary debates (cf.

Shaw, 2000) and courtroom discourse provide further examples of institutional lingual interaction, and there have even been studies of how audience applause — a non-verbal, but certainly lingually meaningful action — in all kinds of settings is both allowed, elicited and achieved (cf. Levinson, 1983:301).

For conversation analysts, however, the central problem was to explain how participants at talk manage in a lingual context that is associational, that is a context in which there is neither accepted authority, nor a more or less durable relationship between the members. 'Durable' refers here to the possibility of the relationship lapsing when a member (terminally) falls away, unlike in institutional relationships, that have a durability beyond the coming and going of individual members. How, in a relationship that is characterized rather by equality between participants, do they manage a lingually economical, and, to bring in a juridical analogy as well, fair way of distributing access to a scarce lingual resource: a turn at talk? What lingual subjects in the communicative event that we call conversation need, as Levinson (1983:297) puts it, is

> ... a sharing device, an 'economy' operating over a scarce resource, namely control of the 'floor'. Such an allocational system will require minimal units (or 'shares') over which it will operate, such units being the units from which **turns** are constructed.

The idea of turn-taking as a set of norms or a system of lingual economy is so deceptively obvious that, before the advent of ethnomethodological analyses, very little attention had been paid to it. Of course, like many other theoretical ideas, the idea of a turn-taking system that is operative in conversation has been strongly contested (for example by O'Connell, Kowal & Kaltenbacher, 1990; Cowley, 1998), but these either proceed from a misunderstanding of the analytical methods and procedures of conversation analysis (cf. for example Sacks, 1984; Schegloff, 1992, 2001) or misrepresent both the positions and the claims made by ethnomethodologists. What is important, however, is neither their critique nor the theoretical endurance of these ideas in spite of their being challenged, but the historical significance of the insight. It is an insight that opened up a dimension of linguistic conceptualisation that we did not have before. The earlier analyses of conversation referred to above (Crystal & Davy, 1969) failed to recognize the potential significance of discovering an organizational structure in conversation, and also the host of explanatory problems that it evokes.

Turn-taking and conversation

One of the hardest questions to answer, if one agrees with the ethnomethodologists, is why it is so that turn-taking is central to conversation. When we look at an actual instance of conversation, it is not difficult to observe that one participant talks, stops, that at that point another starts, talks, stops, at which point the turn at talk is transferred back to the first speaker, and so on.

One possible explanation for this is that in the roughly equal (in the sense of recurrent) distribution of talk across the turns of different speakers there is evidence of the (social) equality of the speakers. Note that, while the notion of lingual distribution is certainly an articulation of an echo of the economic modality (which is originally concerned with the allocation of scarce resources) within the lingual sphere, the idea of equality concerns the social specifications of the role of lingual subjects. The concept of lingual recurrence conceptually echoes the constitutive relation between the lingual aspect and the kinematic. When the opportunity for talk is as evenly and recurrently distributed as in conversation, it is a way of securing, a ratification, of the equality of participants. We shall return below to the idea of ratification or lingual confirmation which, like the idea of lingual accountability, is a juridical analogy within the structure of the lingual aspect.

To see why this explanation is plausible, we need to compare the relatively equal distribution of turns at talk in conversation with other forms of talk that were referred to above. In non-associational, institutional settings for example, there is often a marked and widespread lack of an equal distribution of turns

(Greyling, 1987; Coulthard, 1985; Arthur & Martin, 2006). The lecture is a case in point, for here one of the participants holds forth for almost any length of time, and, moreover, has the ability to withhold from other participants any opportunity of talking, by employing a number of devices: "Let me just finish this point …" is a technique often used to counter an interruption signal from one of the other participants, be it in the form of a cough, a raising of the hand, the clearing of a throat or any combination of these. Actually, it is not so much the size and extension of the turn that suspends the equality of the participants; it is more likely the presence of an authority to allocate (or withhold allocation of) turns. This is probably the case in all institutional settings, even those where one would expect the power gradient between the person who has the authority to influence the allocation of turns and the co-participant at talk to be less steep, as in receptionist-patient exchanges (cf. Hewitt, 2006:142; also 34).

The same inequality seems to reign in law courts, religious services and meetings, where there are either ritualized ways of allocating turns, or where one participant has the acknowledged right to allocate turns (be such a person presiding officer of the court, chairperson, or whatever). There are in these types of discourse signs of the authority relationship that ordinary conversation lacks.

One of the most interesting observations that follows from turn-taking or speaker change in conversation is the remarkable lack of overlap between speakers. It has been calculated that less than 5% — a minimal amount by any standard — of talk overlaps between the turns of ratified speakers (Levinson, 1983:296). In the moment of speaker ratification, we find an echo of a juridical analogy in the lingual aspect: once rightfully confirmed as speaker, and acknowledged as such by co-participants at talk, a speaker has a defensible, allocated space in which to speak. What is even more remarkable about the lack of overlap between speakers is that at the same time gaps between speakers' turns are almost immeasurably small — only a few tenths of a second, and sometimes considerably shorter. In spite of speaker change, talk is therefore continuous, always in progress. This is a significant enhancement of our understanding of the concept of lingual continuity, which is another linguistic primitive, related to the analogical link between the lingual and the spatial dimensions (for a more detailed discussion, cf. Weideman, 2009: chapter 7). It is an illustration of how the constitutive linguistic concept of lingual continuity is enlivened, opened up and developed further by the regulative linguistic ideas that flow from the interconnections between the lingual and the social, economic and juridical analogies. One can therefore, in this further disclosure of the idea of lingual continuity, conceive of it as a communicative space (the turn) in which lingual subjects share expression or meaning in an economically moderated way. This sharing of communicative space is not only a continuous sharing, i.e. one without gaps or overlap, but also the rightful distribution and allocation of it.

An orientation to norms for conversation

How can one explain this? Conversation analysts suggest a rule to which speakers are subject that explains both the absence of gaps between turns and the simultaneous lack of overlap, i.e. the continuity of talk in conversation:

RULE: At least and not more than one party talks at a time

This rule has a normative character, and so does not function as a natural law which is inviolable. Indeed, speakers do in fact overlap (marked //) as in

(1) Desk: What is your last name // Lorraine?
     Caller: Dinnis.
     Desk: What?
     Caller: Dinnis.
                   (Sacks, Schegloff & Jefferson, 1974:702)

but the amount of overlap either remains negligible, or can at least be remedied, as in the above, since both speakers know that a fundamental rule has been violated, and collaboratively set out to rectify such deviation in their first subsequent round of turns. In this lingual collaboration, we see another dimension of the social analogies within the lingual modality. Furthermore, in the normative lingual orientation that co-participants in conversation have towards such violations, we find an illustration of the idea of lingual accountability – speakers set out to rectify and repair the continuity that is to be jointly and collaboratively achieved – which expresses in yet another way the anticipations within the lingual aspect of our experience and the juridical and social.

That knowledge of the rule above is part of our subjective communicative ability or competence is also evident, firstly, in the fact that we know, within milliseconds apparently, that in the case of speakers competing for a turn one has started first. This will probably be the one who will continue while the other drops out, as in

> (2) A: ... I thought he was going to talk us into having to do
>   another complete set of ... set books for that bloody
>   philology // paper
> * B: Erm +
> * A: If he had I'd // have said ...
> * B: the .. the other the other the other + the
>   other man ehm who .. I thought was going to get
>   you wild was Potter.
>   A: (swears) I'll crown that bastard before I'm finished
>   with him.
>   (Svartvik & Quirk, 1980:47, adapted from 786-797;
>   + marks the end of overlap)

Secondly, if there is almost exactly simultaneous talk, we have techniques to snatch a turn or to let it go by either upgrading our tone and pitch, or by fading, as in

> (3) J: But this // person that DID IT + IS GOT TO BE
> * V: If I see the person
> * J: ... taken care of
>   (Levinson, 1983:301)

and

(4) A: .. It is sui generis ..., you see
    B: Yes.
    A: Ehm..
    B: // But I I +
  * A: THIS IS + this is one of the things that eh one of the
        many things eh in English structure which is ehm
        an item in a closed system.
        (Svartvik & Quirk, 1980:46 f., adapted from 738-750)

However interesting these observations may be, ethnomethodology requires that we offer a local explanation for them. If,
as we have remarked, we indeed, as part of our communicative
competence, possess the general ability to recognize and act upon
overlap, while striving to maintain and uphold the fundamental
rule of talk that at least but not more than one party talks at a
time, then it should be obvious that we have some kind of system
for achieving this. For if talk must normatively be continuous,
then, given the fact of turn-taking or recurrent change of speaker,
we must have some means of achieving such change.

How, in other words, do we hand over turns to another in
speaking?

One obvious way of transferring a turn at talk to another
lingual subject is by nominating the next speaker. But while in
other kinds of talk this occurs frequently — cf. parliamentary
debates:

(5) I now call upon the honourable member for Upington ...

or press conferences:

(6) Mr Jackson, from the Daily Star?
— it is clear that speaker nomination has to be done much more
delicately and subtly in conversation. Given the lack of authority
in conversation among equals, it would be ludicrous if in this
kind of talk we are forever being formally and explicitly called
upon to speak. And yet we are called upon to speak, and, if we
reflect upon it, are often selected as next speakers in continuing

conversation, by means of address terms tagged to questions or statements, checks, and so on:

(7) Are you coming, David?
(8) You've been here before, right?
(9) Beg your pardon?

By looking closely at the data, conversation analysts have, however, come up with a whole system of rules to effect speaker change. They have found that turns form units, the ends of which may act as places for transition. These possible completion points are called transition relevance places or TRPs. With this in mind, one may then formulate the rules for speaker change in ongoing conversation by ratified speakers. They are (*C = current speaker; N = next speaker*):

RULE 1 (applying at the initial TRP of any turn):

(a) If *C* selects *N* in his current turn, then *N* and no other must speak.
(b) If *C* does not select *N*, then any party may elect to speak, and the first party to do so has rights to the next turn.
(c) If *C* has not selected *N*, and no other party self-selects under rule l(b), then *C* may, but need not, continue.

RULE 2 (applying at all subsequent TRPs):

When by rule l(c) *C* has assumed the right to take another turn at speaking, then at the next TRP rules 1(a) – 1(c) re-apply, and so on recursively until speaker change is effected. (adapted from Levinson, 1983:298; cf. too Sacks, Schegloff & Jefferson, 1974:704).

These 'rules' are again normative, that is, orientation points or starting places for the collaborative lingual effort we call conversation. It is clear that the rules must be attended to by both *S* (speaker) and *H* (hearer) if they are co-operatively to accomplish a conversational exchange, i.e. transform an *S:H* relationship into a *C:N* one.

Instances of rule 1(a) applying at the first possible completion point for a turn are straightforward enough. Of course, (7) – (9) above will be units at the end of which one may normally expect transition to *N*.

But what about the operation of the other rules? We have, in other contexts, already looked at examples of this, but another clear example of where self-selection occurs is marked * in the following exchanges (the phenomenon marked ** will be discussed below):

> (10) A: Ih .. is .. is it this year that eh Nightingale goes?
>   B: Eh no, next year.
> * A: Ehm sixty / f..
>   B: Sixty five + ..
> ** A: Four, sixty five
>   B: Yeah.
> * A: I thought it was before sixty-five. || So it's not
>   until next year that
>   // the job will be advertised
> ** B: January I suppose there + may be
>   an interview round about January.
>   A: Yeah.
>   (Svartvik & Quirk, 1980:38, adapted from 238-247)

In all the turns marked * in the above, self-selection (as opposed to other, or *C*-selection) has occurred because there are no *N*-selection devices present in the preceding turn, and transition takes place at the end (TRP) of this turn. The operation of rule l(c) is also evident in A's fourth turn (marked ||).

The normative character of rules 1 and 2 also provides, of course, for their violation, as in the intentional interruption

> (11) C: Well, I wrote what I thought was a a .. a reason//able
>   explanation

F: I think it was a very rude letter
                                    (Levinson, 1983:299)

which violates the provision for taking up a turn at a TRP.

Moreover, we have, by virtue of the normative character of these rules, an explanation for significant silences. In (12), A's utterances select B as N, but B, in initially refusing to heed rule l(a) finally yields to the normative force of the rule, which is dependent on the connection between the lingual dimension of experience and the physical aspect of energy-effect, only on his last turn:

(12) A: Is there something bothering you or not?
     (1.0 second gap)
   A: Yes or no?
     (1.5 second gap)
   A: Eh?
   B: No.
          (Levinson, 1983:300)

Apart from explaining why B's "No" probably means "Yes", the rules for achieving speaker change also clarify the sense that lingual subjects, as speakers, have of significant silences. Yet it is astonishing to see how quickly, under normative pressures for conversational continuity, they become so. Silences between turns are not tolerated in this kind of talk, and call up complaints of the kind

(13) You're not listening to me!
(14) C: Mac
     J: Yes
     C: ø
       (2 seconds)
   * J: Hey, trying to waste my time or something?
          (Weideman, Raath & Van der Walt, 1986:97)

121

Since both the fundamental rule for conversation and the rules for achieving change of speaker are normative, they do, as we have seen, allow not only silence(s), but also overlap. The collaborative nature of conversation, however, provides for specific ways of extricating oneself from the chaos that would result if violations were allowed to stand without remedy. There is a kind of lingual retribution, or redress – a clear juridical overtone – at work here. One such remedy, where overlap occurs, is the recycling of the part obscured by overlap, as in (2), (4) and (10) above (marked ** in the latter case), whereby repair is effected.

Repair can also, in the case of inadvertent overlap, be called for in the form of a check, as in Desk's second turn in (1), and effected by the subsequent turn of N.

The existence of possible completion points for turns presents yet another problem not only for Ns, who have to attend to TRPs to avoid complaints in the form of (13), but also for Cs who for some reason wish to hold the floor, i.e. in formal terms, strive to avoid the application of rule l(b) and to continue talking past possible completion points (TRPs) by rule l(c). Thus C may employ what are known as incompletion markers by conversation analysts: 'but', 'and', 'however' constitute devices for temporarily suspending the normative precedence of rule l(b) over l(c). Such markers, however, are only successful in avoiding application of rule l(b) in some instances, as

(15) B: Joe has goh .. got it of course // and
    A: Has he +
  * B: and presumably those are the two people who do it.
        (Svartvik & Quirk, 1980:39, adapted from 324-327)

but not in others:

(16) B: That's what it would amount to, isn't it, but I'd plan to
       get // somebody ...
    A: Well he wouldn't have to hire + somebody you
       see, he'd have you built in.
        (Svartvik & Quirk, 1980:39, adapted from 299-302)

In fact, more than a quarter of all interruptions occur after conjunctions (Coulthard, 1985:64).

Yet other incompletion markers are openings with 'since', 'if', or, more elaborately,

(17) I'd like to make two comments on that. First .... Second ...

Of course, no "incompletion marker" can guarantee that *C* keeps the turn, but they do show up *N* as violating the norm by interrupting, which may be decidedly anti-normative behaviour (see [11] above).

The most sophisticated solutions to the problem of *C* wishing to hold the floor occur before story-telling or jokes. These special incompletion markers are called story-prefaces. Stories and jokes are often begun with

(18) Have you heard the one about ...
(19) There were these three girls ...

The suspension of the rules for turn-taking by story-prefaces calls forth another problem for *Ns*, of course: how do they know that the floor is again open, and that the rules are in operation again?

In the case of jokes the solution is easy, for they have recognizable endings, or punchlines. The laughter that is normative after the punchline paves the way for a resumption of rule-application. But in the case of stories it is of course less easy to perceive endings (which in their turn call for nods, comments, or both) and resumption of talk by rule 2.

In sum: in probing the idea of turn-taking, ethnomethodological analysis has given us an insight into the remarkable normative system that helps us to distribute a factually scarce lingual resource, and one that is 'valued' by lingual subjects – a turn at talk.

A broadening of the concept of objective factual lingual unit

Some of the phenomena of conversation that have been considered in the previous section also concern its lingual wholeness and continuity—specifically the continuous, sequential nature of talk that disallows both gaps and overlap, as well as the beginnings and endings of shorter and longer turns. These two concepts are related, respectively, to the analogies of the numerical and spatial dimensions of experience within the structure of the lingual aspect. It should be obvious that the current discussion significantly broadens and opens up the constitutive notions of lingual objects, restricted as these are to factual units such as morphemes, words and sentences in 'formal' linguistics, that is, in that part of linguistics that attempts to focus and deal exclusively with constitutive linguistic concepts, as these have been defined within the framework employed here.

Let us now consider some remaining questions related to the theme of beginning, continuing and ending in conversation, by asking

- (a) What is the minimum format of the linguistic unit we have been calling a 'conversation'?
- (b) How is this unit begun and ended, and, having arrived at an ending, how can it be re-opened?
- (c) Do we know anything about the overall organization of conversation (for this would be crucial if we wish to understand and probe further its continuity and wholeness)?
- (d) Finally, by what other means is conversation maintained, i.e. not only organizationally (e.g. by rules for change of speaker), but in the efficiency and effectiveness of the content of what is said?

Let us address each of these questions in turn.

A minimum unit for conversation

When, by rule l(a), *C* selects *N* and *N* takes up a turn at speaking, thus fulfilling his or her obligations, these two turns (of *C* and *N*) constitute what we may call a minimum unit of conversational exchange. Most of these units are called adjacency pairs, i.e. they are paired utterances, and exhibit a particular typology of sequence. Thus (initial and closing) greetings are followed by (initial and closing) greetings, questions by answers

(20) A: Eh there was a very nice letter in *The Observer*
on Sunday... I don't know whether you noticed?
B: I didn't see that, no.
(Svartvik & Quirk, 1980: 78, adapted from 1227-1232)

offers and apologies by rejections or acceptances, summonses by answers, complaints by responses, and so on. Again this is an observation that seems quite obviously to match our intuitions about conversational exchanges, but that was first characterized in detail only after receiving the kind of close attention that conversation analysis gave to the data of conversation.

For a conversational exchange to qualify as an adjacency pair, it has to be
(a) two utterances in length
(b) adjacent
(c) produced by different speakers
while the two utterances are moreover to be
(d) sequentially arranged as first and second parts of a
particular typology of sequence (cf. Levinson, 1983: 303).

It is clear, though, that adjacency pairs are only minimum units of conversational exchange. What is more, the requirement of adjacency is often too strong, for conversation analysts have also discovered that in actual data the uttering of a second pair part is often postponed by an intervening 'checking' sequence, as in

125

(21)A: Where do you come from? ⎯⎯⎯⎤
    B: You mean where was I before?⎯⎤ |
    A: Yes.   ⎦ |
    B: History (giggles)   ⎯⎯⎯⎦
       (Svartvik & Quirk, 1980: 152, adapted from 1-5)

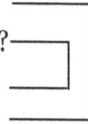

that itself forms an adjacency pair. This postponement of uttering an expected second pair part, however, again stresses the normative organization of conversation: if a second pair part fails to occur, as is normatively expected, the expectation is either retained through the completion of an intervening sequence (technically: an insertion sequence), after which the second pair part occurs, or, in the case of complete failure to occur, it is noticeably absent, as in (12) above.

Opening and closing conversations

This discussion of adjacency pairs as conversational units leads quite naturally to the consideration of the opening and closing of conversations, since the expected initial greeting-greeting sequences ("Hello/Hello") qualify as such units, and so do the closing greeting sequences ("Bye/Bye" or)

(22) B: Thank you very much.
    A: It's a pleasure.
       (Svartvik & Quirk, 1980: 82, adapted from 1460-1463)

Conversation analysis has also discovered that there are sequences (so-called pre-closing pairs) that normally precede closings, as in the turns directly preceding (22) above (single *):

(23)** B: So that's how it goes, um, you know. This bloody university will be the death of me.
    A: Yeah. Oh well. If you inherit a university from bureaucrats what do you expect.
  * A: (laughs)
  * B: Yes...Oh well
       (Svartvik & Quirk, 1980: 82, adapted from 1449-1459)

It appears that our ending of conversations must again be a co-ordinated, collaborative effort, and pre-closing sequences ("Okay...Okay/Right") are a means of achieving this.

Moreover, it has also been discovered that participants in a conversation recognize the transition to pre-closing sections because the turn preceding such a section (cf. the turn marked ** in [23]) is marked by the use of idiomatic and proverbial formulae, or by the reiteration of arrangements already agreed upon

(24) A: See you this afternoon then
     B: Okay

the giving of regards, as well as the proverbial "All's well that ends well" or idiomatic

(25) *   Theresa: Yeah, well, things uh always work out for
                   the best
          Dorinne: Oh certainly
                         (Schegloff & Sacks, 1973: 307)

The normative character of the organizational machinery available for closing a conversation is once again evident in that, having progressed to the closing or pre-closing stages of a conversation, participants can jointly achieve a re-opening. The subject of how such 'closings' can be 'opened' again was indeed the topic of one of the more well-known studies in conversation analysis (Schegloff & Sacks, 1973). In such cases, the reopening bid is usually marked heavily ("Oh BY THE WAY ..."/"HEY LISTEN, I ...").

It follows, from the discussion so far, that what we know today about the opening and closing sections of conversation has also given us a clearer picture of the structure of conversation as a whole, and to this we now turn.

The overall organization of conversation

Conversation analysts have also noted that, having engaged in conversation, we move in a highly ordered way from one topic to another. Thus there are topic boundaries that signal the end of one topic, as well as topic markers that indicate that a new topic is about to be embarked upon, as in

> (26) A: Well that finishes that ehm now what was the other
> thing I wanted to ask you ...?
> (Svartvik & Quirk, 1980: 38, adapted from 236-237)

or in the following, taken from a conversation that had been going on for some time:

> (27) B: I've got a problem for you my lad.
> A: A problem?
> B: Yes.
> (Svartvik & Quirk, 1980: 44, adapted from 601-603)

The literature on topic opening, topic maintenance and topic transition is interesting in its own right, and excellent surveys of the work done are readily available (e.g. Coulthard, 1985). Two final remarks here must, however, suffice for the moment. Firstly, the randomness that stylisticians of a decade or two ago noticed in conversation may have been occasioned in part by the observation of frequent, and sometimes stylistically inexplicable, changes of topic. We know today that such changes are negotiated by means of the complex machinery that is available to speakers.

Secondly, studies have shown that the overall organization of conversation is also normative, in the sense of being a kind of global outline: so speakers may for various reasons skip over some parts, and pay closer attention to others. But we do know that the typical picture that emerges is a progression from one stage to another, and may look something like this (Ferrara, 1980: 332):

(a) initial greeting sequences

(b) howareyou sequences
(c) non-topical sequences
(d) topical sequences
(e) encounter-evaluative sequences
(f) arrangement sequences
(g) closing greeting sequences

The maintenance of conversation

Just as work in conversation analysis has come up with normative explanations for what at first appeared to be the indeterminacy of conversation, so work in pragmatics and speech act theory has enabled us to explain the maintenance of conversation. Specifically, the work of Grice (1975) has shown that participants at talk adhere (throughout) to a general co-operative principle, which says, simply, that in conversation one should typically

(28) Make a contribution such as is required, at the stage
       at which it occurs, by the accepted purpose or direction
       of the talk exchange engaged upon.

Grice goes on to give some further specifications to this norm, particularly the requirements to be

(29) (a) as informative as is required (but not more than is
            required)
       (b) truthful
       (c) relevant
       (d) brief, orderly and clear

Again, as was the case with the rules discovered in conversation analysis, Grice's maxims seem merely to be stating the obvious. Yet they offer an explanation for the existence of non-texts (cf. the doctor/patient exchange discussed earlier, in chapter 4) which appear to violate the maxims on every count. Furthermore, and perhaps more interestingly, the maxims explain the use of phenomena such as irony and metaphor.

Metaphor and irony arise, according to Grice, not when the maxims (29a-d) are merely violated, but when they are *intentionally flouted* by S on the understanding that H will adhere, or interpret *S's* utterance as adhering, at least to the co-operative principle (28), and so understand them as a flouting of one of the maxims. Thus the metaphor

(30) Maggie is an iron lady

will be a flouting of maxim (29b), but by the overriding co-operative principle (28), will be heard as

(31) Maggie is a tough politician

whereas the ironic

(32) She's done a really marvellous job this time, hasn't she?

is, by the same token, heard as

(33) She's messed the car up pretty badly this time, hasn't she?

Conclusion

The conversational phenomena above were discussed within the context of an analysis that focused, first, on the social analogies in the lingual aspect. Second, it considered a number of references within the lingual modality to aspects of experience that lie beyond the social. Specifically, the analysis considered the references that link the lingual aspect of our experience with the economic on the normative side. This analysis has allowed us to conceptualize the turn-taking system discovered by conversation analysts in talk among equals as a device or norm for a shared economy of a scarce lingual resource. This idea of lingual economy includes a notion both of the scarce resource of a turn at talk, and of the distribution of this scarce resource across participants at talk.

The analysis also shows that lingual subjects, in their roles as speakers, have an orientation towards mutuality or collaboration in talk, and towards responding in their formation of lingual objects to a system of norms that allows each enough talking space, and the opportunity to share their expression – often called the "co-construction of meaning" – with selected and ratified others. In the idea of lingual ratification, we have an echo of yet another analogy: the anticipation, within the structure of the lingual aspect, of the juridical sphere. Since the lingual norms we are talking about here are not unbreakable natural laws, but can be violated or intentionally flouted, the analysis has also allowed us to consider what the consequences are when especially the former happens. Since talk is a collaborative communicative achievement, when breakdowns occur as a result of violations of norms for talk, lingual subjects often strive to repair the lingual damage that might cause the communicative event to break down. It should come as no surprise then that the same set of analogies that reflects, within the lingual, the juridical sphere, also allows us to conceptualise the notions of lingual repair, as a means of redress that rectifies and re-adjusts our mutual, collaborative achievements in talk.

Such explanations, together with the insights offered by conversation analysis, convey a sense of the typical normativity – the relative orderliness – of conversation that was impossible to capture by purely stylistic means. If one adds to these the interesting analyses of other kinds of discourse that have been made, one begins to understand why sociolinguistics has today become such a vibrant discipline.

7 A Complex systems approach and language

An emerging new paradigm in linguistics

The selection of linguistic theories and approaches for this book has been influenced by one prime consideration: how likely it would be, for those taking a language like English as a major, to encounter it as an influence in their future professional work with language, or in a field related to language. This means that much that is relevant in other respects has been excluded, and has to wait to be adequately treated and understood. There is little doubt, however, that the approach to language that will be described in this chapter, viz. a complex systems perspective on language, will in the not too distant future become very important for doing linguistics. The same applies to working in one of the language professions. It is an approach that is likely to underlie a great deal of new work that will be done specifically in language teaching, as well as in a number of other fields that are influenced by linguistics and applied linguistic thinking and designs.

Complexity theory has in the recent past emerged as a new paradigm of doing not only applied linguistics (Larsen-Freeman & Cameron, 2008; Cameron & Larsen-Freeman, 2007; De Bot, Lowie & Verspoor, 2007; Kramsch, 2008), but also of gaining a new perspective on language (Beckner, Blythe, Bybee, Christiansen, Croft, Ellis, Holland, Ke, Larsen-Freeman and Schoenemann, 2009). In both disciplines, it represents nothing less than a paradigm shift (cf. Davies 2008: 297). From the perspective of this book, which presents a framework for thinking about linguistics, such shifts are important; when they occur, an opportunity arises to ask a number of questions relating to the foundations of the discipline. Often, linguists and applied linguists are either not interested or do not set aside the time to think about the foundations and the framework of their disciplines. As we have noted in Chapter 1 above, this might make them susceptible either to academic fashion, or to an uncritical acceptance of whatever is proposed.

There are important differences between a complex systems approach and the linguistic perspectives that preceded it. There are also important similarities, or links with current ways of doing linguistics, that we shall take note of. We turn first, below, to an exploration of the main characteristics of a complex systems approach. Before we do, however, there is one important conceptual distinction to be made.

Elementary and complex linguistic concepts

Within the framework for linguistics that has been used in this book, we have so far considered only **elementary** linguistic concepts. These are concepts that derive from the links between the lingual dimension of experience and the other aspects within the modal horizon. These linkages are evident from such elementary concepts as lingual *system*, lingual *range*, lingual *constancy*, lingual *meaning*, lingual *form*, lingual *communication, economy, alignment* and *ratification*, that derive, respectively, from the analogies within the lingual aspect to those of number, space, and movement, as well as the logical, formative, social, economic, aesthetic and juridical modes. Apart from these elementary notions, there is another kind of conceptual instrument: **complex** linguistic concepts. These are concepts that bundle together a whole set of elementary concepts in order to elucidate a phenomenon operating within the lingual sphere.

The three major complex linguistic concepts concern the idea of the relationship between lingual norm and lingual *fact* (that we have already occasionally referred to), the idea that we have of the *origin, growth and maturation* of language (as well as its possible loss in aphasic conditions), and that of the relation between lingual *subject* (users of language) and lingual *object* (the texts or factual lingual units we produce). All of these complex concepts are too multi-faceted to be adequately conceptualised in terms of only one elementary concept or idea. To be understood, they require several: an explanation that is actually a whole set of simultaneous, interacting understandings.

In examining a complex systems approach, we shall investigate one way that linguistic thinking is attempting to come to grips with complex linguistic concepts. This is one of the main reasons why this approach will become even more important in future: it gives us a theoretical angle on lingual phenomena that we have not yet considered, or at least adequately considered, in linguistic thinking.

A complex systems approach

In order to understand the analysis of language offered by a complex systems approach, one must first note how it is understood by its proponents. Their primary starting point is that language has a social origin and function. In this notion, we find the first important difference between a complex systems view of language and that taken by those who subscribe to Chomskyan perspectives on language. As Beckner *et al.* (2009: 2) remark, their views are "radically different from the static system of grammatical principles characteristic of the widely held generativist approach." What this means is that a Chomskyan understanding of language remains a rationalist, and moreover a psychological and biological one, whereas a complex systems view sees language changing and adapting to each new use.

When language is viewed as a complex system, it means that there are *multiple* interacting agents (lingual subjects) that *adapt* and *change* their use of language in such a way that it affects how language then develops and changes in their future interactions. What is more, language use is influenced not only by human *interaction*, and the social processes that are at work when we interact, but also by the cognitive process – and its limitations - through which language is *perceived* by humans. There are multiple factors – physiological, developmental, perceptual, cognitive, social, economic, political - or systems governing them that combine and compete to make language happen. As Beckner *et al.* (2009: 16) point out,

> ... language may change in the tug-of-war of conflicting interests between speakers and listeners: Speakers prefer production economy, which encourages brevity and phonological reduction, whereas listeners want perceptual salience, explicitness, and clarity, which require elaboration.

In this view, the patterns and structures of language arise from the experience that lingual subjects have with language (Beckner *et al.,* 2009: 2). It is the factual experience with language that allows one, when learning a language, to build up a repertoire or set of resources for future language use; grammar is not genetically pre-defined and inbuilt, as in transformational generative grammar, but "a network built up from the categorized instances of language use" (Beckner *et al.,* 2009: 5; cf. too 14).

Evidence for how grammar grows from experience comes from "chunking" phenomena, that we have already referred to before. Not only can and do we learn language by retrieving whole chunks of it from our experience when we need to use them intentionally, but prefabricated sequences of words come in handy also when lingually mature subjects interact: such "frequent word combinations become encoded as chunks" (Beckner *et al.,* 2009: 6). Of course, the use of such lingually meaningful chunks does not mean that language is static. Quite the contrary: even adult grammars can and do change with experience. The main point here is that, in a complex systems approach, grammar develops from language use; humans are acutely sensitive to the frequency with which different structures occur in their language environment (Beckner *et al.*, 2009: 10). Similarly, its understanding of grammar is influenced by the wealth of empirical data now becoming available through language corpora. It follows that its sets of data are therefore potentially much larger than those of the grammars (structuralist and transformationalist) that preceded it.

A good illustration of how language changes through use comes from one of the ways in which the expression of future is handled in English. Since English does not have a future tense, it has to "compensate", as it were, by finding other means or resources to express future intentions, events, and states. The illustration derives from the examination of some of the corpora of English that we now have, some dating back to Shakespeare. In the 850,000 words of his plays, for example, the expression "be going to" occurs only six times, and has no special function (Beckner *et al.*, 2009: 8). In a small corpus of 350,000 words of present day English, however, which is less than half the size of Shakespeare's, its use has grown to 744 occurrences. From signalling merely 'movement' it now takes care also of future intention, and moreover gets contracted into '(be) gonna', a highly productive chunk of language. This happens not only in English, but also in other languages: in 10 out of 76 languages investigated in another study, the expression of future had developed from the verb 'go'. In others, again like in English, where 'will' initially meant 'want', the future derives from a verb initially meaning 'want'. Similarly, the Old English verb 'cunnan' meant only "to know". Now we use its descendant, 'can' as a highly productive auxiliary, and with a much wider intent and meaning. So even words, and word categories, need not remain static, but are drawn into dynamic adaptation processes when used by lingual subjects.

It is evident from the above how the complex systems view depends on a simultaneous and integrated understanding of the concepts of lingual multiplicity (numerical analogy), lingual change and dynamism (reference to the physical dimension), lingual adaptability (organic retrocipation), the process of language use (echo of the physical), lingual perception (reference to the sensitive), grammar and grammatical productivity (formative link), and lingual interaction (social anticipation) (cf. Strauss, 2002 for a similar, and detailed discussion). All these contribute to a number of truly complex linguistic ideas, for example those of language experience (building up a normative resource) that influences future factual language use; and of language change, especially its growth and adaptation.

Complex systems and applied linguistics

A complex systems approach to language is relevant not only for linguistics, but also for applied linguistics. Though there have been other, smaller studies, the pioneering and most ambitious work in describing the relevance of a complex systems approach for applied linguistics is to be found in the recent exposition of Larsen-Freeman and Cameron (2008).

An important tenet of the new approach for them is the non-linearity of the processes of language change that the approach focuses on. If one defines a complex system as one whose behaviour is not predictable in terms of a single dimension, or set of dimensions, but rather emerges from the interactions of its components (Larsen-Freeman & Cameron, 2008: 2), then it follows that the behaviour of a system cannot be predicted in a linear fashion (2008: 72), and that causal explanations, so typical of modernist explanations of phenomena, are no longer sufficient. Rather, since all the various components of a complex system (including what previously was sometimes inappropriately sidelined as 'context') are in continuous interaction, there is what they call "reciprocal causality" (2008: 7, 60). The processes of language change can therefore be described as a "movement in a trajectory across a 'state space' or 'phase space'" (2008: 20, 43). The change process, if drawn towards a sufficiently powerful 'attractor' (2008: 20), can come to a provisional stability. An example of this is when certain emergent patterns of language use become temporarily stable around the strong attractor of the notion of a standard language (2008: 81).

In any development of language, therefore, there are valleys or troughs, that act as attractors, with sides that are either steep or less steep. It is across such a topological landscape (Figure 7.1, below, from Larsen-Freeman & Cameron, 2008: 53) that one may plot the growth and development of a complex system such as language. From a complex systems perspective, the growth, and the path and trajectory of such growth, can never be merely linear.

Should the state of a language, finding itself in the trough of a strong attractor such as a standard language, be such that it becomes stable, it should still be noted, however, that the emergent patterns that a complex systems approach finds are relative stabilities. Complexity theory acknowledges that no system is wholly free of change, since the many interacting components of systems each bring their own measure of instability and thus unpredictability with them. So even small changes that are introduced into a system can have dramatic effects, spreading 'through the system, diluting the determinism and rendering the outcome of system activity unpredictable' (Larsen-Freeman & Cameron, 2008: 75).

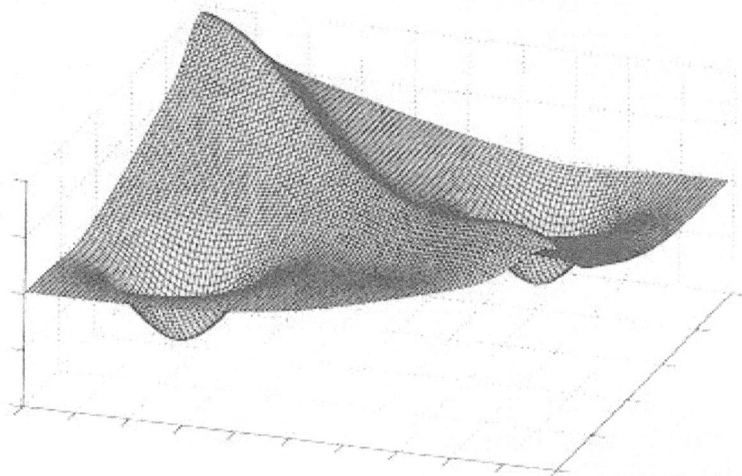

Figure 7.1: A topological landscape for plotting growth of a complex system

For growth to occur, change must happen. It follows that, when there are no strong attractors (deep troughs or valleys) in the trajectory of development of language, as in Figure 7.2 below, language learning is easier. When the attractor is strong, however, as in the case of a first language whose patterns continue to confuse and prevent learners from gaining complete fluency in a second or third language, as in Figure 7.3, we have a case of learning being much more difficult.

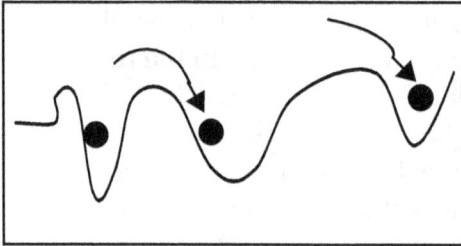

Figure 7.2: Easier and   **Figure 7.3**: More difficult development

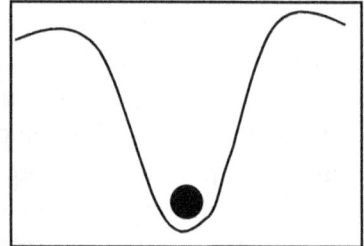

How learning and growth can happen in the face of what is called here "strong attractors", such as first language usage and patterns of sound formation, grammar and meaning, is of course a problem for language pedagogy. This is the reason why applied linguists are directly concerned with the identification and discovery of regular patterns, both in language and in learning. The grammatical subsystem of a language is just one such recurrently regular pattern (Larsen-Freeman & Cameron, 2008: 84). Language develops, from a complex systems perspective, in a process of co-adaptation, that gives rise to an alignment of patterns between, for example, learner and interlocutor (2008: 127). This development becomes even more complicated when the learning is that of a second or third language, and the conflicting and competing patterns and regularities of different languages have long been of interest to applied linguistic analyses.

Before we consider an example of how this kind of insight can assist us in designing language teaching interventions, we should first note how prominent the biotic terminology is in a complex systems analysis and discussion: even the relationship between accelerated lexical growth and grammatical development is described in organic concepts, as two subsystems that are connected growers (Larsen-Freeman & Cameron, 2008: 149). So, too, we should note, learning a language is seen as language development rather than as acquisition, as a process of dynamic adaptation (2008: 157) rather than as something that, once learned, is "possessed" for all time. In the same way, discourse and discourse types are viewed as multiply interconnected complex systems, and the language-using patterns that each discourse type yields are a resource of language potential that is actualised in each instance of talk or text creation within such a system (2008: 174). So, for instance, the expectations that derive from previous experiences of co-creating language with others, and of so aligning oneself with the latent meaning potential of others through discourse, as these have been identified, for example, by conversation analysis, become 'attractors', or locations of relative stability for language use in such contexts (2008: 179; cf. too 193). In the same fashion, written texts can be viewed as co-constructed, yet asynchronous, collaborative compositions, in which writers imaginatively engage with, and thus interact with, prospective readers (2008: 188).

Learning language in the classroom

As regards learning language in the classroom, a complex systems approach emphasises, as we have seen above, that even small interventions can make a big difference. What then are the new design principles for language teaching that the approach can contribute, especially to learning in the language classroom?

In one excellent illustration of a complexity perspective on a how a classroom task was accomplished, Larsen-Freeman and Cameron (2008: 204f.) describe how to interpret the variation on a language task, both in terms of language use and the potential to grow the potential resources at the disposal of learners. The task in the example required of Norwegian learners to nominate and then discuss an arctic animal in English. By making use of the concept of an *interaction differential*, they measure the difference between the demand from the teacher (from open requests, the most demanding, to closed questions, the least demanding) and the responses from the learners, that range from minimal (the least desirable) to more expansive (the most desirable) offerings.

As we noted above in the analysis of classroom discourse in Chapter 5, new and unconventional methods of language teaching make for different patterns of interaction between teacher and learners in the language classroom than those in the traditional language classroom, where the learners have minimal chances to speak and use the language. The patterns of language use in the unconventional classroom are assumed to be more beneficial for learning, since they maximise learner opportunity to speak. Similarly, in the example given here, the design of the language task is intended to give learners the maximum opportunity to speak and use the language.

The interactive talk between the teacher and individual learners is carefully plotted, turn by turn, in terms of such opportunities for learners to use the language. The relative size of the opportunity is then expressed in terms of an inter-action differential. The analysis shows that the trajectory of the interaction in most cases goes from a high (and therefore pedagogically meaningful) differential towards the powerful, but pedagogically less helpful attractor of a low differential, as especially the teacher leads a process of co-adaptation that will ensure at least some measure of success on this language task. In one significant case, however, the trajectory does not slide into this less desirable stable condition. This is where a learner chooses an animal of which he indeed has some knowledge, and on his own initiative increases the interaction differential.

This interpretation is significant for the design of language tasks. It is evident that, in tasks like these, if the teacher beforehand ensures an increase in the prior content knowledge of the learners about the topic of the discussion, the interaction differential may increase, and so stretch the potential latent language resources of the learners. As the authors remark (Larsen-

Freeman & Cameron 2008: 212), activities in the language class would enhance the potential of learning and growth of learners' language if they can be designed "to challenge learners to exploit the meaning potential of their developing systems in new ways."

A perennial problem for language teaching has been the 'fossilization' of language at some stage in learners' development. This is a concept that implies exactly what it says: learning a second language might progress until it becomes frozen, as it were, and unable to reach its native-like target. Complexity theory also enables new interpretations to be given to previous observations on such fossilization of language. We can now look at a learner's stage of acquisition of an additional language, long considered to be an interlanguage (Selinker 1972), a kind of waystage on the path to the desirable end of (almost) native-like competence in the target language, as a language ability in the grip of a "strong attractor". Rather than taking a cross-sectional view of language as in the "interlanguage" perspective, however, a complex systems approach can plot the path of individual growth and variation across a time-scale (Larsen-Freeman & Cameron 2008: 245). Moreover, the earlier explanations for fossilization must yield, in a complex systems perspective, to an acknowledgement of the "boundless" potential to grow one's language resources, and not stop at the powerful attractor that is "the neural commitment of the first language, and the ensuing entrenchment, [that] may lead to a deep valley or well" (2008: 142), which constitutes a trough in the trajectory of learning an additional language.

In this kind of view, teachers and language course designers can also find an explanation not only for individual variation, but also of apparent lapses in language learning. In two telling further examples, Larsen-Freeman and Cameron (2008: 135f.) show how individual growth may vary in terms of fluency, vocabulary complexity and grammatical complexity for a number of language learners, and how, in a single learner, there may be both growth and lapses. Since these learners are seen as organisms that are free to explore new behaviours (2008: 148), and since language growth does not follow a linear path, a complexity theory explanation can readily provide an interpretation for a phenomenon that many teachers will attest to. How is it, one often hears language teachers ask, that learners sometimes 'unlearn' or simply fail to learn elements of the target language that they should, by linear expectations, already have possessed or acquired?

In a complex systems perspective the many interacting subsystems of language, and the abilities of learners in terms of components of this whole, such as discourse practices and structure, grammatical patterns, vocabulary resources, as well as the various other interacting dimensions, like interventions and language demands in specific contexts, provide an explanation for non-linear growth in learners' language. The essence of this explanation lies in the variation in any one or more parts of these interacting systems. Any one factor or effect may change the state of development of a language learner.

From a language task design angle, this means that a complex systems approach would make applied linguists more sensitive to the varying demands and levels of learning that can sometimes be found in a single classroom. As these authors put it (Larsen-Freeman & Cameron, 2008: 226):

> ... language resources of individuals exist only as latent potential to engage in appropriate patterns of interaction until realized in specific discourse environments... The challenge is for interaction, tasks and tests to be designed, planned, and managed so as to push and stretch an individual's language resources to the edge of their current potential.

The approach clearly has the potential, through the emergentist view of language learning that it takes, to realise this view in designs for language teaching.

A critical assessment

In viewing language as a complex, open interplay of multiply interacting elements and forces, such as cognition, consciousness, experience, human interaction, society, culture and history, that jointly either amplify or limit the effects of these components, this approach allows us to see all of these as connected (Beckner *et al.*, 2009: 18). If everything is connected, an important corollary of this view is then that the perspective is anti-reductionist, and from this comes much of its opposition to the reductionism of modernist approaches to science. Modernist reductionism usually seeks a single modality as the sole or main explanatory principle for all phenomena. In modernist linguistics, the single, absolutised modality has varied with each new paradigm: for structuralists, everything depended on lingual position and relation, a clear singling out of the spatial mode. In generativism, the human mental faculty became absolute. Throughout its history linguistics has been characterised by such explanatory one-sidedness. It is this that is opposed by a complex systems analysis of language.

Yet, somehow, in spite of this intention, a complex systems view also seems to retain the modernist tendency to reduce explanations to a single dimension of reality. As Larsen-Freeman and Cameron (2008: x, 5) make clear, complex systems thinking finds its roots in biology. It is not surprising, then, that its key concepts revolve around the adaptability (2008: 33) and potential of systems, especially the ability to self-organise (2008: 62), and "the organic nature of change" within those systems (2008: 1; 17). In the same way, the focus of the new approach on constant, dynamic, ongoing change is one that is related in the first instance not to a physical, but to a biotic understanding of things: "… an organism's ongoing activity continuously changes its neural states, just as growth changes the physical dimensions of the body", these authors remark (2008: 17; cf. too 29, 32, 72). We should note, however, that the emphasis is not as much on analogical physical concepts, such as dynamic effect or power, as on analogical biotic conceptualisations of phenomena (cf. too Strauss, 2006: 149f., and 2009: 62 for a similar conclusion regarding the intellectual pioneer behind systems theory, Von Bertalanffy). Phrased differently: the flux that is the focus of the approach is interpreted in an organically dynamic way.

It is clear that a complex systems approach therefore wrestles with the age-old question of how to explain the sometimes remarkable stability of a continuously changing system; to explain, to put it another way, the systematicity or orderliness of a system. It sees the explanation in the analogically biotic notion of adaptability:

> If we are seeking an explanation of how 'order' ... comes to be in complex adaptive systems, then we may find it in thinking of a complex system that is flexible enough to maintain its stability through continuous adaptation. (Larsen-Freeman & Cameron 2008: 56; cf. too 36)

To its credit, it should be said that, by taking a transdisciplinary approach, a complex systems view stretches across the boundaries of cognitive psychology and sociolinguistics. It borrows methods and concepts from studies as diverse as those of finger movements (Larsen-Freeman & Cameron, 2008: 208). It reinforces and gives fresh interpretations to, or devises new uses for some of the more conventional current approaches such as conversation analysis (Chapter 6, above), discourse studies (Chapter 5, above), ethnographic description (Larsen-Freeman & Cameron, 2008: 242), action research (2008: 244), cognitive linguistics (Breckner *et al.,* 2009: 15; cf. Langacker, 1987, 1991; Dirven & Verspoor 1998) and corpus linguistics.

Furthermore, it exposes, though now from another perspective than the conventional objections that have been raised, some of the shortcomings of language course designs that assume linear growth in learners' language using potential. At the same time, it sets itself apart from postmodernism, whose

> response to over-simplification of the world through a focus on entities is to fragment and disperse, to deny wholeness by making it multiple, hybrid, and difficult to grasp. Complexity theory, in contrast, embraces complexity, interconnectedness, and dynamism, and makes change central to theory and method. (Larsen-Freeman & Cameron 2008:1)

The exponents of a complex systems approach downplay the natural scientific bases of complexity theory, probably because those kinds of connections have in the past, especially in modernist conceptions of applied linguistics, tended towards technocratic analyses and solutions for language problems, and are currently unfashionable. Be that as it may, possibly because it has not yet had enough time to influence linguistic and applied linguistic conceptualisation, a complex systems perspective clearly has links with the natural sciences in at least two senses: its emergentist and biotic starting points, and its reliance on technical modelling of language change and development. As Breckner *et al.,* (2009: 12) confidently declare, they consider mathematical or computational modelling as a valuable tool in their analyses.

From a philosophical point of view, the main contribution of a complex systems approach lies in its attempt to offer a non-reductionist perspective to language and language learning and teaching (Larsen-Freeman & Cameron 2008: 231, also 16, 40f., 72). In such a perspective the absolutisation of a single dimension is, in principle, avoidable. The critical question that adherents of the new approach would have to answer, however, is whether one might not perhaps call the emergentism, that seems to lie at the bottom of its conceptual offering, itself a reduction. Phrased differently: is the strong emphasis on organic analogies, though novel, not itself another (over)simplification of things lingual?

In defence of its anti-reductionist stance, proponents of a complex systems view may point to its attention to other than biotic analogies. So for example, its analogical physical conceptualisations of language dynamics, or analogical psychical identification of lingual volition (Larsen-Freeman & Cameron, 2008: 157), together with its emphasis on the numerical analogy of a multiplicity of systems, certainly all add additional, non-biotic, dimensions to its perspective. Similarly, in its identification of how the subjective, normative ability or potential that humans have for creating language (2008: 104; 226), which are notions related to the formative analogy within the lingual dimension of our experience, correlates with the factual resources that are at the disposal of language-using agents, it touches on yet another set of analogical lingual concepts. Indeed, the approach is in my estimation a genuine attempt at investigating and analysing what in this foundational framework would be categorised as "complex" (in distinction from merely complicated, or elementary) concepts. Complex linguistic concepts are notions that that view phenomena such as language growth and loss, lingual subject and object, and lingual norm and lingual fact from a multiplicity of analogical conceptual angles.

Does a complex systems view provide us with a sufficient perspective on complex concepts? Perhaps not, as Larsen-Freeman and Cameron (2008: 14) graciously acknowledge; complexity theory, according to them, needs to be complemented by other theories. What does concern me still is that the authors are hesitant to acknowledge that the predominantly organic analogies of complexity theory are more than merely metaphorical (2008: 11f.). I find this unnecessary, especially in view of their treatment of all the other analogical concepts, such as dynamism, openness, self-organisation, adaptation, emergence and system as apparently non-metaphorical and unproblematic. A lingual system, for example, if defined, as I have done in this book, as a unity within a multiplicity of lingual norms or patterns that correlate with a vast variety of factual lingual phenomena, is no metaphor, but a conceptual, analogical link between the lingual and numerical dimensions of experience.

The opposition of complexity theory to rationalist conceptions of human lingual ability gives the impression that its focus is more strongly on empirical, factual data of language use (cf. Larsen-Freeman & Cameron 2008: 219, for example), an impression that is enhanced by its meticulous analyses of actual language events, and its reliance on large corpora of data, as well as new interpretations of older research, done from the vantage point of previous paradigms.

The new approach is likely contribute to new designs for language teaching, as has been pointed our above. It is likely to make us, as the designers of new solutions, more sensitive than before to current and emerging webs of interacting social, administrative, and political systems. As these interacting systems co-adapt in response to social and other pressures, freshly designed solutions in offering language instruction also emerge. The most important contribution of postmodernism to our understanding of language teaching issues has been to make us more sensitive to political interests in education. The approaching intellectual fashionability of a complex systems approach may perhaps give us a new angle on how to deal with these issues, and take us beyond postmodernism.

8 Linguistic primitives as framework for linguistics

Paradigm differences in linguistics

What is important in understanding the theoretical argument for presenting a framework for linguistics in this book is to recognise that this framework in the first instance serves to account for the strong and weak points of the various competing and complementary approaches to doing linguistics. Moreover, it should be clear from the preceding explanations that each current and new approach to how linguistic analysis should be done is informed by some theoretical or philosophical starting point. In this way, early approaches to formal linguistics were structuralist, before they were superseded by the mentalist perspectives of Chomskyan rationalism. The latter was challenged by Halliday's systemic functional grammar (SFG), which, as the following excerpt from an interview with Halliday makes clear, was Marxist in orientation. On the occasion of the S. Pit Corder commemorative colloquium at the 2007 annual conference of the British Association for Applied Linguistics (BAAL), Halliday was asked about his beliefs, and how these influenced his linguistic theory (Davies, Joseph & Weideman, 2007: 3). Here is the question and his answer:

> *AW*: ... I ask this question simply because I'm interested in what happens to people at historical turning points. To me, your own work created a bridge between theoretical linguistics and social perspectives on language at a time when the discipline was badly in need of it. My question is this: At that time, did you see its importance for the historical development of the discipline? Did you have any inkling of how influential it would be? Or did you simply do it out of sheer conviction? ...

> *MH*: ... I just would like to put together four components. One was simply personal conviction. One can look into background reasons for that. It could be connected with all sorts of things like my father being a dialect specialist in Yorkshire. But secondly and most importantly, there's my background as a student of Firth, because of course for J.R. Firth the link between theoretical linguistics and social perspectives was central. You couldn't do linguistics unless you put it in that sort of context, and I took on that view from Firth. Thirdly was my own background as a Marxist and work with our little linguistics group in the Communist Party in the fifties. We were searching for a Marxist linguistics and that obviously had to be grounded in a social context....

Wherever one turns in linguistics, one is confronted, therefore, by –isms: the relationism of the structuralists, as well as their behaviourism; the cognitivism and mentalist roots of generativism; the Marxism underlying the systemic choices in SFG; the emergentism and organicism of a complex systems approach. This kind of overemphasis is rife in theoretical explanations across all disciplines; the skewed perspective it brings is not limited to linguistics. Many practical reasons are given for such absolutisation. One is that it brings back a necessary balance in perspective. Thus, feminism, as it allies itself with later developments in (critical) discourse analysis, is seen as the necessary corrective of sexism and paternalism. Likewise, the over-emphasis on political power that is embedded in critical analyses of all kinds, also in postmodernist perspectives in applied linguistics, is regarded as repairing the damage of colonialism and racism. And in the latest development, a complex systems approach, we have a critique of rationalist and generativist starting points that counters these in empiricist and organicist terms.

Despite these plausible reasons, the perspective of this book is that such emphases spring from the convictions that underlie the various analyses. Of this the confession by Halliday in the interview excerpt above is a good illustration. We were first alerted to the risks of such absolutisations by postmodernism. Postmodernism itself is, at least in the case of applied linguistics, opposed to this kind of reductionism, hence its emphasis on fragmented perspectives and on the real and potential abuses of political power. Yet it seems, from the perspective of this book, to be fighting fire with fire, which, ironically, calls up the attendant danger of its own perspective being consumed by the relativism it uses as analytical tool to create disenchantment with analytical and philosophical bias in other theories. If the relativist starting point, viz. that everything is relative, were true, then it must apply, of course, to everything *except* that starting point. The starting point itself has to be exempted from relativity, which makes it meaningless or untrue in its own terms. Most recently, and subsequent to postmodernist critiques, a complex systems approach has in its own way and on its own terms alerted us to the dangers of reductionism. Yet it too, as we noted above, has its own favourite and preferred starting point in the organic mode of reality, a preference that of necessity has to exclude certain other modes of explanation.

The main problem that I see here, therefore, is that while all the different paradigms in linguistics may in their own terms be internally more or less consistent, and, hence, intelligible, their internal consistency and intelligibility as starting points for understanding language are no guarantee that they could, as theoretical vantage points, robustly explain the connections that they have with the other traditions and paradigms that operate within the discipline. In fact, as different perspectives, they are quite likely to constrain, compete with and suppress the others, even while co-existing with them (McNamara, 2008: 304). We must not forget that different disciplinary traditions are more often than not institutionalised, and derive organisational power from the contexts in which they are embedded. Such power may well be resistant to change, or at least create an unwillingness to offer room for alternative theories or philosophies to grow.

Linguistics cannot function without a philosophical base

The existence of competing and complementary paradigms in linguistics is part of the history of linguistics. When we try to sanitise the discipline by obscuring paradigmatic differences and promoting 'consensus' views, we end up with a bland semi-understanding of the discipline. That does a disservice to new entrants into the field. There is a remedy for such blandness and the risks attached to presenting only half of the story to those entering the discipline. It lies in acknowledging that linguistics – like all other disciplines, in fact – needs a philosophical framework that will allow one to weigh and assess the various emphases in its history of successive paradigms. What McNamara (2008: 304) points out with regard to applied linguistics as a discipline applies equally to linguistics itself:

> It is important to keep alive an understanding of the theoretical perspectives that have been proposed in the past so that their enduring relevance is appreciated and we do not go on reinventing the wheel... Historical amnesia is a persistent temptation in a(n)... intellectual field...

The development of a robust and systematic foundational framework for linguistics, a foundation that addresses and articulates the philosophical bases of the field, is therefore inordinately important. By revealing their modal and perceptual biases, such a framework as the one presented here not only gives us an insight into the workings of previous and current paradigms, but also provides us with a theoretical way of accounting for new paradigms that may arise within linguistics. Of the latter, the discussion of a complex systems approach to language in the previous chapter is a good illustration.

How the understanding that McNamara (2008) proposes must be accomplished, however, and what measure of accounting for and appreciating "enduring relevance" we should have, is, of course, never a given. So the theoretically robust framework that the discipline of linguistics is in need of should ideally be able to clarify and explain all of the different paradigms that have influenced the discipline. Such a framework must of necessity be one that stands beyond the parochial defence of its own theoretical starting points, and the effects of taking a single experiential mode above all others as first principle. It must reach beyond both the history of linguistics, and the biases that are associated with its various paradigms.

It is a pity that work within a discipline rarely connects with the foundations of that discipline or with other fields. Such connections can be established by building deliberately on a theoretical framework. One of the important contributions to linguistics of a complex systems approach is that it has again sensitised us to the possibility of seeking a theoretical framework for linguistics in a transdisciplinary or philosophical foundation. There is no doubt that the foundational framework that linguistics needs is philosophical in nature, and this has consequences for how we view, from the vantage point of linguistics, the other disciplines that relate to it. There are increasingly calls for breaking down the walls that currently separate disciplines, especially the disciplinary boundaries within the humanities. We cannot do so, however, without a philosophical or transdisciplinary base.

Yet we should not limit the task of "breaking down the walls" to those separating the human sciences only. If we are to adopt a more comprehensive, foundational framework for linguistics, we need to refer not only to the human or cultural dimensions of our experience, as linguistics has done, especially in venturing beyond formal linguistics into investigating sociolinguistic ideas. Of course, the disclosure of the lingual dimension of our experience by social, economic, aesthetic, juridical and other modes yields regulative linguistic ideas that have greatly enriched our understanding of things lingual, as we noted especially in chapter 6 above. Yet the references in linguistics to the natural dimensions of experience – its numerical, spatial, kinematic, physical, organic, and sensitive modes, as well as to the cultural dimensions such as the logical and formative aspects, which in their conceptual relationships with the lingual mode offer to us constitutive linguistic concepts – are the building blocks of linguistic theory. Linguistics connects both with human and with natural sciences (Weideman, 2009).

Linguistic primitives

The accomplishment of the desired framework for linguistics in this book proceeds from the notion of basic linguistic concepts or theoretical primitives. The various analogies of other aspects within the lingual dimension of experience that we have considered here illustrate that these references allow us to conceptualize some basic or foundational phenomena that have traditionally been investigated by linguistics. Taken together, these basic concepts form a class of linguistic primitives or foundational theoretical concepts in linguistics that provide us with a framework to pursue the investigation of lingual phenomena not in a piecemeal, but in a single, coherent, and integrated framework. Since they are foundational concepts, this means that linguistic primitives are, in essence, founding concepts of the discipline, and, in that sense, philosophical. Though they are linguistic concepts, they derive a good deal of their meaning from a coherent foundational or philosophical perspective. This philosophical framework was developed by Dooyeweerd (1953), and derives especially from his idea that reality has a horizon of modalities that allows our theoretical analysis to conceptualize a multiplicity of unique, mutually irreducible, yet interconnected aspects. By viewing these modalities as irreducible but interconnected, Dooyeweerd's approach in principle avoids the reductionist pitfalls that impede theoretical concept-formation whenever one mode of reality is absolutised, and all others are subsumed under it.

In linguistics, there is a long line of investigation that, to a greater or lesser extent, has attempted to utilize this framework by showing how the lingual mode of experience, which defines the field of investigation of linguistics, coheres or analogically reflects all the other aspects of reality: the numerical, spatial, kinematic, physical, organic, sensitive, logical, formative, social, economic, aesthetic, juridical, ethical and confessional. The analogical connections of the lingual aspect with earlier (foundational or constitutive moments) and later aspects (generating regulative ideas) yield, upon analysis, a number of linguistic primitives. In a recent analysis done in terms of such a framework (Weideman, 2009), I have, following Hommes (1972) and others (De Jongste, 1949, 1956; Verburg, 1951, 1965, 1971, 1976; Strauss, 1967, 1970, 1971; Yallop, 1978; Weideman, 1981; Bakker, 1984), presented a much more detailed foundational articulation of various such linguistic 'primitives' or elementary systematic concepts of linguistic theory than in this introduction, but the framework employed in both is the same.

The main concepts and ideas of the analysis are summarized below in tabular form (Table 8.1). So far, these have been presented as successive modalities in a series that is arranged horizontally, in a sequence that echoes their being earlier and later modalities in an order of time. It is important not to misinterpret their presentation below, in Table 8.1, as hierarchical, or an order of higher and lower. The sequence remains one of earlier and later aspects; the numerical is not 'higher' or 'lower' than the ethical, nor does it have less value. The same applies to the aspect of belief and those that precede it, if one turns the table upside down. Trust is not higher or more valuable than frugality, which characterizes the economic mode of reality.

Table 8.1: Constitutive concepts and regulative ideas in linguistics

Disciplinary angle	Aspect/function/ mode to which lingual refers	Analogical links	Kind of concept yielded
	numerical	system and unity within multiplicity	foundational constitutive concepts
	spacial	range & relation	
	kinematic	constancy and movement	
	physical	effect & process	
	organic	differentiation & adaption	
	sensative	volition and perception	
	analytical	meaning and identity	
	formative	command and forms	
lingual	**nuclear moment/**	*expression related to understanding of signs*	
	social	types of discourse and communication	disclosing regulative ideas
	oconomic	scarcity and distribution	
	aesthetic	alignment and co-construction	
	juridical	ratification and redress	
	ethical	accountability and integrity	
	confessional	commitment and trust	

Generally, such foundational notions as are placed in the theoretical spotlight by the analysis of the analogical link between the lingual and other experiential aspects may be characterised either as constitutive concepts or as regulative ideas. The examples of the links or analogies between the lingual and the aspects preceding it belong to and generate the set of elementary linguistic concepts, and are called retrocipations. In that sense the numerical, spatial and kinematic aspects are 'earlier' aspects than the lingual, and such concepts are, by that token, constitutive. Those connections between the lingual dimension of reality and the aspects following it, on the other hand, are elementary linguistic ideas or limiting, approximating – in the sense of concept transcending – notions. They derive from analogies in which the lingual anticipates, and is disclosed by the social, economic, juridical, ethical and confessional dimensions of reality. Since these are subsequent or 'later' aspects in relation to the lingual, a systematic investigation of their coherence with the lingual will only be able to grasp that linkage in terms of a set of anticipatory moments, from which is derived a set of limiting concepts or regulative linguistic ideas.

The historical and the systematic

A framework for linguistics such as that attempted in this book has both a systematic and a historical side. Its starting point is that the systematic concepts yielded by the interconnections between the lingual and other dimensions are closely linked with the history of the discipline.

Therefore, the concepts that have been surveyed above are more often than not of significant historical interest: compare, for example, the notion of lingual system (as in work from De Saussure to Chomsky and Halliday's SFG, and beyond them to complex systems theory); that of lingual position and sequence (as in structuralist linguistics); and the concepts of lingual constancy and movement (as in transformational grammar). Less obvious, perhaps, but equally important are notions of lingual spheres of discourse, text type and lingual acceptability that normally fall within the purview of the linguistic sub-disciplines of pragmatics, discourse analysis and text linguistics. The analysis has demonstrated that such systematically and historically important and influential concepts are related to the coherence between the lingual dimension of reality, which delimits the field of study of the discipline of linguistics (Weideman, 1981, 2009), and other aspects of reality, such as the numerical, the spatial, the kinematic, the logical, the formative, the social, and so forth. As we have noted, the notion of lingual system that De Saussure was so influential in identifying, articulates the coherence between the lingual and the numerical: a system of lingual norms is a unity within a multiplicity of norms. Similarly, the factual position and sequence of lingual elements, as this was explicated in the work of the structuralists, provides evidence of the connection between the lingual and the spatial dimensions of our world. The notion of lingual constancy (and also the regular positional movement of lingual elements) is an analogy that lies at the heart of transformational grammar, and relates to the link between the lingual dimension of reality and the kinematic. If we take as a final example the analysis of the social anticipations in the structure of the lingual aspect (an analysis that yields a linguistic idea), we encounter notions of lingual spheres of discourse, each with their own normative requirements that variously determine the factual lingual text types that operate within them, and ideas of lingual acceptability within a differentiated number of spheres of discourse (cf. Weideman, 2009: chapter 14).

No doubt, similar analogical concepts may be discovered in other, more recent approaches to linguistic conceptualization. Cognitive linguistics (Langacker, 1987; 1991; Dirven & Verspoor, 1998), though by its own admission an approach that is not part of mainstream linguistics (Langacker, 1987:v), is one such approach that echoes many of the concerns that are articulated in the foundational framework that I have been working from. Apart from its concerns with "the conceptual clarification of fundamental issues" (Langacker, 1987:1), its attention to the notions of expressive (lingual) extension (space) and how we perceive and cognitively process objective lingual facts in terms of semantics and syntax is without doubt of importance to a foundational linguistic analysis. A similar case can be made for the importance of SFG, that builds upon the work of Halliday (1985), and that has barely been touched on here (chapter 2). The insights of SFG form a very important bridge across a major fault line in linguistic theory also oriented to in cognitive linguistics: that between formal linguistics and sociolinguistic analyses. To do justice to such approaches, they need serious and separate treatment, which falls outside the scope of this introduction. Similarly, the minimalist turn that transformational grammar has taken (Chomsky, 1995), though ostensibly concerned with notions of economy and simplicity as conditions for universal grammar (Chomsky, 1995:168-171) may be of interest in that respect, but is not as accessible as the Chomskyan analyses discussed above in chapter 2.

Another assumption made in the articulation of the framework for linguistics in this book, and that I have sought to illustrate in the analysis offered above, is that constitutive elementary linguistic concepts and regulative linguistic ideas are interdependent. In the development of a systematic linguistic methodology, the investigation of constitutive linguistic concepts must be complemented both by an enquiry into regulative linguistic ideas, and by a systematic linguistic analysis of the various complex linguistic concepts. Moreover, the conceptual understanding of one set of such linkages or analogies is not really possible without either implicit or sometimes explicit reference to other analogies. This is most clearly seen in the analysis of a complex systems approach to language that was the subject matter of chapter 8, above.

Possibly the strongest argument in favour of employing a deliberate theoretical framework such as the one articulated here is that through it, one is able to set up lines of communication among various competing or potentially complementary paradigms within linguistics. Again, it should be said to the credit of a complex systems approach that it attempts to revive older methodologies, such as conversation analysis and ethnographic description, blending them with newer methods related to computer modelling of language use, and the study of linguistic corpora. However, selecting from the older methodologies what is useful, and discarding what is not, requires reference to criteria that can only be credible if they can be justified in terms of a theoretical framework. There is thus an interplay between the history of the discipline, and the systematic treatment, appraisal and assessment of previous, current and new paradigms. I would claim that doing linguistics without a systematic framework that allows one to assess the varying emphases, excesses and *lacunae* of different schools of linguistic thought sets one up to fall victim to the implicit beliefs embodied in them. Like all other scientific disciplines, linguistics is a human undertaking, with all of the normal risks that human action entails. Furthermore, if postmodernism has taught us one thing, it is that we should not ignore the drivers of power behind institutional forces, and the biases and prejudices that such institutional power brings. And science is done within institutions. This book is therefore an attempt to create intellectual space for useful and alternative views of how disciplinary work may be accomplished, and to establish meaningful communication among the various schools of thought within linguistics. Its commitment is to doing linguistics responsibly.

BIBLIOGRAPHY

Allerton, D.J. (1979) *Essentials of grammatical theory: A consensus view of syntax and morphology.* London: Routledge & Kegan Paul.

Arnold, D.J. & Bennet, P.A. (1982) *Revised Extended Standard Theory: An overview and guide.* Unpublished manuscript.

Atkinson, J.M. & Heritage, J. (eds.) (1984) *Structures of social action: Studies in conversation analysis.* Cambridge: Cambridge University Press.

Arthur, J. & Martin, P. (2006) Accomplishing lessons in postcolonial classrooms: Comparative perspectives from Botswana and Brunei Darussalam. *Comparative education* 42(2):177-202.

Bakker, D. (1984) Kritische notities bij Ferdinand de Saussure's Cours. *Philosophia reformata* 49(1):1-34.

Beckner, C., Blythe, R., Bybee, J., Christiansen, M.H., Croft, W., Ellis, N.C., Holland, J., Ke, J., Larsen-Freeman, D., & Schoenemann, T. (2009) Language is a complex adaptive system: Position paper. *Language learning* 59 (supplement 1):1-26.

Berry, M. (1975) *An introduction to systemic linguistics, 1: Structures and systems.* London: Batsford.

Brown, G. & Yule, G. (1983) *Discourse analysis.* Cambridge: Cambridge University Press.

Burton, D. (1980) *Dialogue and discourse: A sociolinguistic approach to modern drama dialogue and naturally occurring conversation.* London: Routledge & Kegan Paul.

Butler, C.S. (1985) *Systemic linguistics: Theory and applications.* London: Batsford Academic and Educational.

Cameron, L. & Larsen-Freeman, D. (2007) Preview article: Complex systems and applied linguistics. *International journal of applied linguistics* 17(2):226-240.

Carrell, P.L. (1982) Cohesion is not coherence. *TESOL quarterly* 16(4):479-488.

Carstens, A. (2009). *The effectiveness of genre-based approaches in teaching academic writing: Subject-specific versus cross-disciplinary emphases.* Unpublished D. Phil. thesis. Pretoria: University of Pretoria.

Chomsky, N. (1957) *Syntactic structures.* The Hague: Mouton.

Chomsky, N. (1975) *Reflections on language.* New York: Pantheon.

Chomsky, N. (1979) *Language and responsibility: Based on conversations with Mitsou Ronat.* Brighton: The Harvester Press.

Chomsky, N. (1982a) *Rules and representations.* Oxford: Basil Blackwell.

Chomsky, N. (1982b) *The generative enterprise; A discussion with Riny Huybregts and Henk van Riemsdijk.* Dordrecht: Foris.

Chomsky, N. (1995). *The minimalist program.* Cambridge, Massachusetts: The MIT Press.

Clark, H.H. & Clark, E.V. (1977) *Psychology and language: An introduction to psycholinguistics.* New York: Harcourt Brace Jovanovich.

Cook, V.J. (1978) Second-language learning: A psycholinguistic perspective. *Language teaching and linguistics: Abstracts* 11 (2):73-89.

Cook, V.J. (1985) Chomsky's Universal Grammar and second language learning. *Applied linguistics* 6(1):2-18.

Coulthard, M. (1985) *An introduction to discourse analysis.* Harlow, Essex: Longman.

Cowley, S. (1998) Of timing, turn-taking, and conversations. *Journal of psycholinguistic research* 27(5):541-571.

Craig, R.T. & Tracy, K. (eds.) (1983) *Conversational coherence: Form, structure and strategy.* Beverly Hills: Sage Publications.

Crystal, D. (2003) *The Cambridge encyclopedia of the English language.* 2nd edition. New York: Cambridge University Press.

Crystal, D. & Davy, D. (1969) *Investigating English style.* London: Longman.

Davies, A. (2008) TESOL, applied linguistics, and the butterfly effect. Contribution to Symposium: Theory in TESOL. *TESOL quarterly* 42(2):296-298.

Davies, A., Joseph, J., & Weideman, A.J. [transcription by K. Mitchell]. (2007) The Pit Corder colloquium: Interview with Michael Halliday and Ruqaiya Hasan. *BAAL 2007 conference proceedings:* 3-10. Edinburgh: University of Edinburgh.

De Beaugrande, R.A. (1980) The pragmatics of discourse planning. *Journal of pragmatics* 4:15-42.

De Beaugrande, R.A. & Dressler, W.U. (1981) *Introduction to text linguistics.* London: Longman.

De Bot, K., Lowie, W. & Verspoor, M. (2007) A dynamic systems theory approach to second language acquisition. *Bilingualism: Language and cognition* 10(1):7-21.

De Jongste, H. (1949) Taalkunde en taalbeschouwing. *Philosophia reformata* 14(1):3-42; (2):49-57.

De Jongste, H. (1956) On symbols. *Philosophia reformata* 21(4):162-174.

Dirven, R. & Verspoor, M. (1998) *Cognitive exploration of language and linguistics.* Amsterdam: John Benjamins.

Dooyeweerd, H. (1953) *A new critique of theoretical thought.* 4 volumes. Amsterdam: H.J. Paris.

Duff, P.A. (2002) The discursive co-construction of knowledge, identity and difference: An ethnography of communication in the high school mainstream. *Applied linguistics* 23(3):289-322.

Edmondson, W. (1981) *Spoken discourse: A model for analysis.* Harlow, Essex: Longman.

Ferrara, A. (1980) Appropriateness conditions for entire sequences of speech acts. *Journal of pragmatics* 4: 321-340.

Givon, T. (1979) From discourse to syntax: grammar as a processing strategy. (In Givon, T. ed. *Syntax and semantics 12: Discourse and syntax.* New York: Academic Press. P. 81-112).

Gleason, H.A. (1961) *An introduction to descriptive linguistics.* New York: Holt, Rinehart and Winston.

Goffman, E. (1981) *Forms of talk.* Oxford: Basil Blackwell.

Greyling, W.J. (1987) *The typicality of classroom talk and its relevance for the training of teachers.* Unpublished M.A. dissertation. Bloemfontein: University of the Orange Free State.

Grice, H.P. (1975) Logic and conversation. In (Cole, P. & Morgan, J.L. eds. *Syntax and semantics 3: Speech acts.* New York: Academic Press. P. 41-58).

Habermas, J. (1970) Toward a theory of communicative competence. (In Dreitzel, H.P. ed. *Recent sociology 2,* London: Collier-MacMillan. P. 115-148).

Halliday, M.A.K. (1978) *Language as social semiotic: The social interpretation of language and meaning.* London: Edward Arnold.

Halliday, M.A.K. (1985) *An introduction to functional grammar.* London: Edward Arnold.

Halliday, M.A.K. & Hasan, R. (1976) *Cohesion in English.* London: Longman.

Hartnack, J. [tr. M. Holmes Hartshorne] (1968) *Kant's theory of knowledge.* London: MacMillan.

Hendricks, W.O. (1973) *Essays on semiolinguistics and verbal art.* The Hague: Mouton.

Heritage, J. & Atkinson, J.M. (1984) Introduction. In Atkinson, J.M. & Heritage, J. eds. 1984:1-15.

Hewitt, H. (2006) Front desk talk: A study of the interaction between receptionists and patients in general practice surgeries. D. Phil thesis. Edinburgh: The University of Edinburgh. [Online]. Available http://www.era.lib.ed.ac.uk/handle/1842/1482. Accessed 22 September 2007.

Hjelmslev, L. [tr. F.J. Whitfield) (1963] *Prolegomena to a theory of language.* Madison, University of Wisconsin Press.

Hommes, H.J. Van Eikema. (1972) *De elementaire grondbegrippen der rechtswetenschap: Een juridische methodologie.* Deventer: Kluwer.

Hymes, D. (1971) On communicative competence. (In Pride, J.B. & Holmes, J. eds. *Sociolinguistics: Selected readings.* Harmondsworth: Penguin P. 269-293).

Joos, M. (1966) Preface. (In Joos, M. ed. 1966:v-vi).

Joos, M. (ed.) (1966) *Readings in linguistics, Volume 1; The development of descriptive linguistics in America 1925-56.* Chicago: Chicago University Press.

Kemper, S. & Thissen, D. (1981) Memory for the dimensions of requests. *Journal of verbal learning and verbal behavior* 20:552-563.

Kramsch, C. (2008) Ecological perspectives on foreign language education. *Language teaching* 41(3):389-408.

Langacker, R.W. (1987) *Foundations of cognitive grammar 1: Theoretical prerequisites.* Stanford, CA: Stanford University Press.

Langacker, R.W. (1991). *Concept, image and symbol: The cognitive basis of grammar.* Berlin: Mouton de Gruyter.

Larsen-Freeman, D. & Cameron, L. (2008) *Complex systems and applied linguistics.* Oxford: Oxford University Press.

Levinson, S.C. (1983) *Pragmatics.* Cambridge: Cambridge University Press.

Lyons, J. (1969) *Introduction to theoretical linguistics.* Cambridge: Cambridge University Press.

Lyons, J. (1970) *Chomsky.* Glasgow: Fontana/Collins.

Matthews, P.H. (1981) *Syntax.* Cambridge: Cambridge University Press.

McNamara, T. (2008) Mapping the scope of theory in TESOL. Contribution to Symposium: Theory in TESOL. *TESOL Quarterly,* 42(2):302-305.

O'Connell, D.C., Kowal, S. & Kaltenbacher, E. (1990) Turn-taking: A critical analysis of the research tradition. *Journal of psycholinguistic research* 19(6):345-373.

Palmer, F.R. (1976) *Semantics: A new outline.* Cambridge: Cambridge University Press.

Radford, A. (1981) *Transformational syntax: A student's guide to Chomsky's Extended Standard Theory.* Cambridge: Cambridge University Press.

Reichling, A. 1947. De taal: Haar wetten en haar wezen.
(In Reichling, A. & Witsenelias, J.S. eds.
*Eerste Nederlandse systematisch ingerichte
encyclopaedie* 2. Amsterdam: ENSIE).

Richmond, J. (1982) *The resources of classroom language.*
London: Edward Arnold.

Robins, R.H. (1967) *A short history of linguistics.* London:
Longman.

Sacks, H. (1984) Notes on methodology. In Atkinson, J.M. &
Heritage, J. eds. 1984:21-27.

Sacks, H., Schegloff, E.A. & Jefferson, G. (1974) A simplest
systematics for the organization of turn-taking for
conversation. *Language* 50(4):696-735.

Sampson, G. (1980) *Schools of linguistics: Competition and
evolution.* London: Hutchinson.

Schegloff, E.A. (1992) On talk and its institutional occasions.
(In Drew, P. & Heritage, J. eds. *Talk at work:
Interaction in institutional settings.* Cambridge:
Cambridge University Press. P. 101-134).

Schegloff, E.A. (2001) Discourse as interactional achievement
III: The omnirelevance of action. (In Schifrin, D.,
Tannen, D. & Hamilton, H.E. eds. *The handbook
of discourse analysis.* Oxford: Oxford University
Press. P. 229-249).

Schegloff, E.A. & Sacks, H. (1973) Opening up closings.
Semiotica 8:289-327.

Searle, J. (1969) *Speech acts: An essay in the philosophy of
language.* London: Cambridge University Press.

Seerveld, C. (1980) *Rainbows for the fallen world.* Toronto:
Toronto Tuppence Press.

Selinker, L. (1972) Interlanguage. *International review of applied
linguistics* 10:209-231.

Shaw, S. (2000) Language, gender and floor apportionment in political debates. *Discourse & society* 11(3):401-418.

Sinclair, J. McH. & Coulthard, R.M. (1975) *Towards an analysis of discourse: The English used by teachers and pupils.* London: Oxford University Press.

Smith, R.N. & Crawley, W.J. (1983) Conjunctive cohesion in four English genres. *Text* 3(4):347-373.

Storch, N. 2004. Using activity theory to explain differences in patterns of dyadic interactions in an ESL class. *Canadian modern language review* 60(4):457-480.

Strauss, D.F.M. (1967) *Wysgerige grondprobleme in die taalwetenskap.* Bloemfontein: Sacum.

Strauss, D.F.M. (1970) *Wysbegeerte en vakwetenskap.* Bloemfontein: Sacum.

Strauss, D.F.M. (1971) *Wetenskap en werklikheid: Oriëntering in die algemene wetenskapsleer.* Bloemfontein: Sacum.

Strauss. D.F.M. (2002) The scope and limitations of Von Bertalanffy's systems theory. *South African journal of philosophy* 21(3):163-179.

Strauss, D.F.M. (2006) *Reintegrating social theory.* Frankfurt am Main: Peter Lang.

Strauss, D.F.M. (2009) *Philosophy: Discipline of the disciplines.* Grand Rapids: Paideia Press.

Svartvik, J. & Quirk, R. (eds.) (1980) *A corpus of English conversation.* Lund: CWK Gleerup.

Svennevig, J. (2001) Abduction as a methodological approach to the study of spoken interaction. [Online]. Available http://home.bi.no/a0210593/Abduction%20as%20a%20methodological%20.pdf. Accessed 2 October 2007.

Van Els, T., Bongaerts, T., Extra, G., van Os, C. & Janssen-van Dieten, A. [translated by R.R. van Oirsouw] (1984) *Applied linguistics and the learning and teaching of foreign languages.* London: Edward Arnold.

Van Heerden, C. (1965) *Inleiding tot die semantiek.* Johannesburg: Willem Gouws.

Van Jaarsveld, G.J. & Weideman, A.J. (1985) *Doelgerigte Afrikaans: Boek I.* Bloemfontein: Patmos.

Van Langevelde, A.P. (1997) Bilingualism and economic development in west European minority language regions: A Dooyeweerdian approach. [Online]. Available http://irs.ub.rug.nl/ppn/162991215. Accessed at http://som.eldoc.ub.rug.nl/FILES/reports/1995-1999/themeC/1997/97C39/97c39.pdf on 22 October 2007.

Van Langevelde, A.P. (1999) Bilingualism and regional economic development. A Dooyeweerdian case study of Fryslân. *Netherlands geographical studies* 255. Groningen: Utrecht/Groningen Royal Dutch Geographical Society/Faculty of Spatial Sciences University of Groningen.

Verburg, P.A. (1951) Enkele lijnen en feiten in de ontwikkeling der taaltheorie. (In Zuidema, S.U. ed. *Wetenschappelijke bijdragen door leerlingen van Dr D.H. Th. Vollenhoven.* Franeker: Wever. P. 13-32).

Verburg, P.A. (1965) Delosis and clarity. (In Fortman, W. F. de Gaay, Hommes, H.J., Dengerink, J.D., Langemeijer, G.E., Mekkes, J.P.A., Van Peursen, C.A. & Stellingwerff, J. eds. *Philosophy and Christianity: Philosophical essays dedicated to Prof. Dr. H. Dooyeweerd.* Kampen: Kok. P. 78-99).

Verburg, P.A. (1971) De mens in de taalkunde. (In *Truth and reality: Philosophical perspectives on reality dedicated to Prof H.G. Stoker.* Braamfontein: De Jong's. P. 262-282).

Verburg, P.A. (1976) The idea of linguistic system in Leibniz. (Offprint from Parret, H., ed. *History of linguistic thought and contemporary linguistics.* Berlin: Walter de Gruyter. P. 593-615).

Visser, S.F. & Weideman, A.J. (1986) A measure of texture: Cohesion in English radio drama dialogue and actual conversation. Pre-published in *Textures* 2:1-18; SA *Journal of linguistics* 4(4):90-100.

Waher, H. (1984) Chomsky se teorie van 'Government-Binding'. *SPIL plus* 9.

Weideman, A.J. (1981) Systematic concepts in liguistics. MA dissertation. University of theFree State, Bloemfontein.

Weideman, A.J. (1984) General and typical concepts of textual continuity. *SA Journal of linguistics* 2(1):69-84.

Weideman, A.J. (1985a) *Making certain: A course for advanced learners of English.* Bloemfontein: Patmos.

Weideman, A.J. (1985b) Discovering conversational units. *Acta academica* New Series B(2):195-207.

Weideman, A.J. (1985c) Teaching the future teachers: from the analysis of classroom talk to the development of materials. *L.A.U.D.T. Papers* B 142. University of Duisburg.

Weideman, A.J. (1988) *Linguistics: A crash course for students.* Bloemfontein: Patmos.

Weideman, A.J. (2009) *Beyond expression: A systematic study of the foundations of linguistics.* Grand Rapids, MI: Paideia Press in association with the Reformational Publishing Project.

Weideman, A.J., Raath, J. & Van der Walt, P.J. (1986) Continuity and discontinuity in talk: Some brief notes on summonses. *SA journal of linguistics* 4(4):90-100.

Weideman, A.J. & Verster, L. (1988) "Two roads diverged ...": an analysis of the achievement of partings. *SA journal of linguistics* 6(4):55-68.

Wells, R.S. (1966) De Saussure's system of linguistics. In Joos, M. ed. 1966:1-18.

Yallop, C.L. (1978) The problem of linguistic universals. *Philosophia reformata* 43(1&2):61-72.

www.ingramcontent.com/pod-product-compliance
Lightning Source LLC
Chambersburg PA
CBHW020458030426
42337CB00011B/152